THE CHURCH ON THE HILL

AN ACCOUNT OF THE CHURCH, PEOPLE, AND PARISH OF BUCKFASTLEIGH

HELEN HARRIS

DEVON BOOKS

First published in Great Britain by Devon Books

British Library Cataloguing in Publication Data

A CIP record for this book is available from the British Library

ISBN 0 86114 907 6

DEVON BOOKS
Official Publisher to Devon County Council

Halsgrove House
Lower Moor Way
Tiverton
Devon EX16 6SS
Tel: 01884 243242
Fax: 01884 243325

The front cover illustration is a painting of Buckfastleigh Church by P.O. Hutchinson, 31 July 1880. (Courtesy Devon Record Office). The ruins of the medieval chapel lie to the right of the church and the Cabell tomb to the left. The back cover photograph shows the church on its prominent hilltop position with the abandoned Bulley Cleaves Quarry visible in the foreground.

Printed in Great Britain by The Devonshire Press, Torquay.

CONTENTS

ACKNOWLEDGEMENTS

The author gratefully acknowledges the help given by the following:
Mr W Ballard
Miss H Beard
Mr S Blaylock
Buckfastleigh Town Council
Mrs R Child, English Heritage
Mrs E Churchward
Mr R Clutterbuck
Dr J. Cox
Devon County Record Office, Exeter
Devon County Sites & Monuments Register
Mrs L Full
Mr J G Gill
Mr and Mrs R Gill
Miss D Griffiths, Dartmoor National Park Authority
Mr P Hamilton-Leggett
Detective Chief Inspector M Howard, Devon & Cornwall Constabulary
Miss E Knowling
Mr J Knowling
Mrs R Look
Professor Nicholas Orme
Mrs J Sanders
Mrs J Soul
Mr J Voisey, Blight & Scoble
Mr R Weekes
Westcountry Studies Library
West Devon Record Ofice, Plymouth
The Revd Paul Wilson, Vicar of Buckfastleigh 1991-96
Particular thanks are due to Simon Timms who provided much valued help and encouragement throughout the preparation of this book.
Individual photographs are acknowledged to their source. All other photographs are from the author's collection.

✒ INTRODUCTION ✒

The Church of the Holy Trinity, Buckfastleigh, serenely situated on the limestone hill north-east of the little town, has, for centuries, stood as a landmark to travellers approaching from almost any direction. Witnessing to generations of christian worship on the site, the substantial building and its proud spire may evoke a variety of emotions, both to those familiar with it and to new-comers - of thankfulness, of welcome, and of inspiration.

For over seven hundred years it was to the church here that parishioners came to attend services, to receive Word and Sacrament, to be joined in matrimony and to bury their dead. They ascended from the town itself - the industrial settlement that grew up along the banks of the Mardle - by climbing either one of the steep lanes, or the 196 Church Steps. They came too from the nearby village of Buckfast, and from the farming country that stretches from the River Dart westwards to the hills of Dartmoor.

Although it has always been the successions of people themselves who have formed the Church - the Body of Christ - in this place, the ancient church building stood as the focal point of their worship and fellowship and was revered, cherished, and lovingly cared for. In this sublime position, with views extending over hills and woodlands to the moor, and the tranquil atmosphere within its walls, one somehow felt that much 'nearer to heaven'.

From time to time over the ages Holy Trinity Church has suffered the effects of unfavourable forces. At this elevation extremes of weather could be harsh on the fabric. In 1849 a fire was started in the vestry, causing damage and destroying the parish chest. During the Second World War blast from bombs that fell nearby shattered some of the stained glass windows. And occasionally there were incidents of theft and petty vandalism. But, on the night of 20-21 July 1992, a far more vicious attack was wreaked upon the building in the form of an act of arson. The fire soon gained a hold, and despite valiant efforts the roof and interior structures were destroyed, and the outer walls rendered unsafe. The hearts of many people were similarly smitten and stunned.

Thus made totally unusable, the building's blackened shell was wired off for safety reasons and openings necessarily boarded up to prevent unauthorised access. Although damaged, the tower and spire remained standing, and the bells were removed and given sanctuary at Buckfast Abbey. Experts were called in to advise, and work done towards making safe the ruined walls and in rescuing certain remnants within, including those of the fine Norman font whose shattered pieces have, with great skill, since been reassembled.

Following the sad event, services were transferred to Buckfastleigh's chapel-of-ease - the smaller St Luke's Church[1], built in the town a century previously for the convenience of townspeople who found the ascent difficult, and used hitherto particularly for early morning and winter evening services.

Work has proceeded in restoring the solid parts of the church which survived the fire. The tower and spire have been repaired, the bells re-hung, and other structures made good. After a period of chaos, a semblance of order, even tranquility, now prevails in this noble shell, deprived of its roof and thus open to the skies. As yet the future for Holy Trinity is uncertain, but many hope that a way may be found for worship to be resumed on the site. Such is the faith of those who abhor defeat by the evil of arson, and who strive for new life in this long-established holy place.

See page 93 for notes on the Introduction.

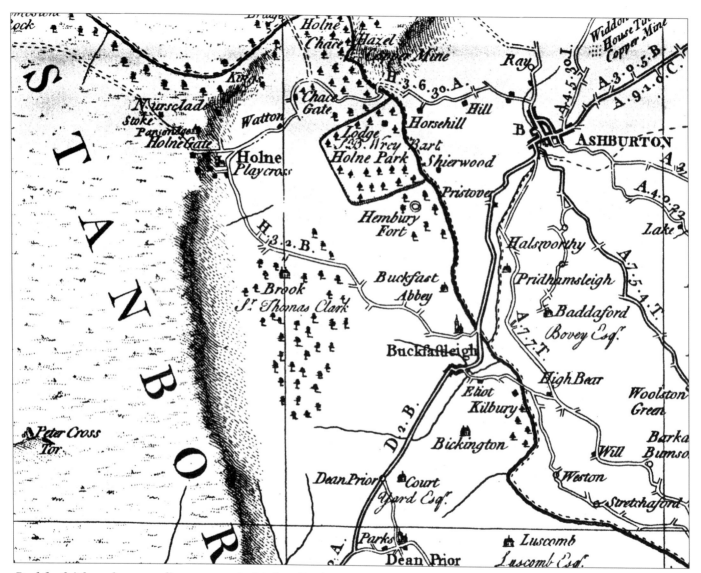

Buckfastleigh and surrounding area as depicted on Benjamin Donn's Map of Devon, dated 1765.

6

1
⁂ THE PARISH OF BUCKFASTLEIGH ⁂

The parish of Buckfastleigh,[1] fringing the south-east of Dartmoor, as seen on the map appears roughly kite-shaped, with its length extending west to east. The distance along this axis is five and a half miles, the greatest width from north-east to south just over three miles, the eastern boundary nearly two miles, and the western border about one mile in length.

There are marked variations of altitude, and of the type of countryside. On the east, where the River Dart forms the boundary separating Buckfastleigh from the parishes of Ashburton and Staverton[2], the land is little more than 100ft above sea level. From the valley the hill of Devonian limestone on which the church is sited rises steeply to over 200ft. The main areas of population are in the eastern sector of the parish: the village of Buckfast north of the hill, Buckfastleigh town to the south-west. Westwards the undulating land forms a series of hills, some farmed, some pleasantly wooded, interspersed with deep lanes and streams, and this gives way to moorland which ascends to a level of 1,690ft at Petre's Bound Stone on Ryder's Hill. The moors of this western extremity comprise around 1,000 acres, and Buckfastleigh is one of twenty-two border parishes which share a boundary with the Forest of Dartmoor, as defined by an official perambulation in the year 1240. (The term 'forest' does not here denote a covering of trees, but relates to it having been a royal hunting ground. For many years forming part of Lydford parish, the central area of high moor, which is part of the Duchy of Cornwall, is now identified parochially as 'Dartmoor Forest'. The moorland areas within the surrounding parishes were constituted as the 'commons of Devon' and certain farms in these parishes have carried entitlements to

Petre's Boundstone on Ryder's Hill stands at a height of nearly 1700 feet.

grazing and other rights in the forest [venville] as well as on their own moors).[3]

On its south side the ancient parish of Buckfastleigh shares a short boundary with Rattery parish, and then, proceeding west, a longer one with Dean Prior, which is defined for some of its way by the Dean Burn, and for a distance on the moorland, to the summit of Puper's Hill, by the line of an ancient reave (a prehistoric land boundary). Along the north side Buckfastleigh is separated from Holne parish by the infant River Mardle (see over) and then, farther east, by the Holy Brook.

Early inhabitation of the area is evident from the prehistoric remains on the moor, which include an enclosed homestead known as Mardle Ring sited on the valley side, containing circular hut remains.[4] Off

The river Mardle forms the medieval parish boundary with Holne, in an area where many prehistoric remains can be found.

the moor, in Hembury Wood,[5] are substantial remains of an Iron Age hill fort.

There was probably little penetration by settlers of the largely wooded in-country until the Saxons came westward in the seventh century AD. Subsequent centuries have seen a sustained flow of in-comers, although with losses of population, too, such as those caused by the Black Death from around 1349.

Farming, of course, has been a principal form of occupation in the parish from very early times, with pastoral systems, of sheep and cattle, predominating at the higher levels. By the middle of the twelfth century tin-working had became an important activity on Dartmoor, and was well-developed by the time Buckfastleigh Church was in being. Parts of Buckfastleigh Moor were worked in this way. The earliest dates for tin extraction here are not known, but certainly as time progressed operations proceeded around the sources of the Wella Brook and the Mardle and on the slopes of Snowdon, and included open workings such as Gibby's Beam and Snowdon Hole. There may have been working for iron, and later copper was mined in the parish, at Brookwood in the nineteenth century and in a smaller mine at Combe. At Wheal Prosper, in woods between Wallaford Down and the Dean Burn, tin was sought during the 1800s.[6]

A view of the parish in the late 1750s may be gained from a questionnaire completed by the then vicar of Buckfastleigh, the Revd Robert Bradford, in response to a request from Dean Milles of Exeter who was planning to write a comprehensive history and sent out forms to all incumbents in the diocese.[7] Concerning agriculture, replying to a question on how the land was improved, the vicar wrote: 'By lime, and dung. 12 hogsheads of lime and 160 seams (horse-loads) dung to each acre is good dressing'. Grains grown were said to be wheat, barley and oats. On the quantity of acres under orchards, Mr Bradford replied: 'We have many acres but the number I can't say'. On apple varieties he looked on 'Whitsower' as the best. Cider was certainly widely made in the parish, but on the quantity made yearly the vicar wrote: 'Very variable'. On its quality he replied: 'Is remarkable for its goodness if well managed'. Regarding woodland, the total acreage for the parish was given as 'about 600 acres'. This was chiefly of coppice, with oak thriving best, and King's Wood was noted as being of about 300 acres, almost all of oak. (Oak bark was important for the local tanning industry and, probably a little later, wooden soles for Lancashire are believed to have been made in King's Wood, where they would be stacked to dry before dispatch).

Livestock bred in the parish were said by Bradford to be 'Black cattle and pretty large flocks of sheep', mostly sold at Buckfastleigh, Brent, Ashburton, and Totnes markets. The mention of black cattle is interesting and would suggest this as the colour of the

Remains of granite extraction on Puper's Hill.

indigenous cattle before the South Devon breed was fully developed.[8] The South Devon, which probably owes its golden-red colouration and other characteristics to a cross channel influx of bloodlines, became the customary summer-grazing animal on the moor. (The early black cattle were not of the same breed as those of that colour commonly seen on Dartmoor today which are mostly Galloways, a breed not introduced here until the late nineteenth century). The sheep were probably of the Whitefaced Dartmoor type.

Buckfastleigh parish was well endowed with rocks usable as building material. Out on the moors granite

- or moorstone as it was earlier known - was readily available, and there is visible evidence of it having been worked on a small scale, even since 1800, near the summit of Puper's Hill. Farther east, the hill of Devonian limestone on which the church was built has been quarried at various locations. The stone has been widely used throughout the town in the construction of buildings and in numerous walls. These, in early summer, support colourful flowers of pink valerian and blue ivy-leaved toadflax, which have colonised and become established in the mortar over many years. There was considerable industry in the burning of limestone in kilns, with lime-sand mortar being the most common bonding agent for building until the introduction of cement. Besides also being employed in industries such as tanning, a further important use for the lime was, as already said, on the land, to reduce acidity in the soil and improve its structure. The largest of these quarries was Black Rock or Bulley Cleaves,[9] close to the Buckfast road, where a form of black 'marble' was also extracted. Bulley Cleaves Quarry eventually closed in February 1974. A special feature of this limestone is the occurrence of extensive caves, in which have been found bones of large animals long extinct in this country. One of the caves actually extends directly under the church itself. (See page 69).

The older of the two main settlements is, in fact, Buckfast. The year 1018 is now regarded as the likely date when the first Benedictine Buckfast Abbey was founded here, in the reign of King Canute.[10] In 1086, as recorded in the Exeter Domesday Book, the abbey was endowed with a manor of about 300 acres called Bulfestra (as Buckfast was - perhaps erroneously - there spelt), as well as with other manors located more distantly. The name 'Buckfast' is probably derived from 'fastness, or stronghold, of the deer'. For the following fifty years or so the abbey was apparently somewhat in eclipse,[11] until in about 1136, during the reign of King Stephen, it was given to the Abbot of Savigny in Normandy. Savignac monks were installed at Buckfast, and then, after just eleven years, in 1147, they were absorbed into the Cistercian Order, under whose occupation the life of the abbey continued for four centuries, until the Dissolution of the Monasteries in 1539. (See Chapter three.).

The Cistercians followed the Rule of St Benedict in its more austere form. They were deeply involved in farming, particularly of sheep for wool, and their activities must have greatly influenced the area. It was probably as trees on abbey property were felled and its meadows extended, and land was made available for cultivation, that Buckfastleigh - the 'clearing' of Buckfast - came into existence, with the bounds of the parish undoubtedly defined by the year 1300. The earliest known documentary evidence for the Church on the Hill dates from the thirteenth century, with the

Urban District   of Buckfastleigh

CIVIC BALL

At The Town Hall, Buckfastleigh

On FRIDAY, 26th NOVEMBER, 1971

RECEPTION 7.15 p.m.   SUPPER 8 p.m.

Dancing to 1 a.m.

Royal Marines Dance Band, Dartmouth

Ticket £1.75

REFRESHMENTS   LICENSED BAR

The parish church and the features that gave Buckfastleigh its name were depicted on the crest of the Urban District Council, as this Civic Ball invitation from 1971 depicts.

first vicar, Walvanus, installed under the patronage of the Abbot and Convent of Buckfast with the approval of the Bishop of Exeter, in 1263 (see Appendix 1). There may have been a place of earlier pagan ritual here - it was not uncommon for Christian worship to become established on such a former site.

On the Dissolution the abbey lands became the property of the king. The manor of Buckfast was initially rented by Sir Thomas Dennys, who had been the abbey's chief steward - representing it in civil matters and in the manorial courts - before being bought by him. It appears that in 1541 a dispute arose, and was taken before King Henry VIII in Council, between the inhabitants of Buckfastleigh and Sir Thomas Dennys concerning the venville grazing rights on the moors of Holne, Buckfastleigh, and Brent, which Dennys was trying to deny them. He was also keeping them from digging and taking marl from the quarry near the church, and forbidding them the use of a fair for butter, and of a pathway from the town to the church.[12] The manor remained in the Dennys family until about 1700, following which it was held by the Bakers and the D'Oyleys before being sold in various parcels.[13]

The manor of Buckfastleigh remained in Crown hands until 1629 when it came under the ownership of a Ralph Freeman. After Freeman's death in 1634 the moiety of the manor of Buckfastleigh was bought by the (second) Richard Cabell, and on his death was inherited by his son (the third) Richard in 1655.[14] It was this third Richard who built the manor house at Brook in 1656, and the prominent 'sepulchre' for the family tomb opposite the south door of Holy Trinity Church. The first Richard Cabell had come to Devon from Frome, in Somerset, following his marriage to Susannah Peter, daughter of John Peter of Buckfastleigh, probably in the later years of the sixteenth century. In the early 1600s he evidently possessed a manor in the parish called Maynbow, or Mainbow, which it appears may have been concurrent with that described as Brook.

The third Richard Cabell died in 1672 and his estates were inherited by his young daughter Elizabeth. Twenty years later she married a baronet's son, a bigamist, Cholmeley D'Oyley. After his death she married, in 1702, Richard Fownes, and although she was advanced in years they had a son, Thomas. A law-suit, which resulted in Elizabeth having to pay a substantial marriage settlement in respect of her late husband to his father, Sir John D'Oyley (who shortly inherited Buckfast Abbey) caused severe financial problems to the couple. They both died in the 1730s. Their son Thomas lived at Brook Manor, but in 1758 sold 'the manor of Brook Mainbow with Buckfastleigh and Button' to Sir Thomas Clarke, Master of the Rolls, who left it in his will to the Earl of Macclesfield.

The Cabells were regarded with suspicion and fear by people in Buckfastleigh and stories were perpetuated about them and their tomb in the churchyard. A well documented account of the Buckfastleigh branch of the family has been given in the booklet researched and written by Susan Cabel Djabri, a descendant of another line.

In his reply to Dean Milles' questions in the 1750s the Revd Robert Bradford noted the manors of Buckfastleigh parish as: Buckfastleigh, Mainbow, Kilberland, and Buckfast. White's Directory of 1878 stated that the Earl of Macclesfield was lord of the manor of Brook Mainbow with Buckfast and Button and that he owned a great part of the parish. The manor of Buckfastleigh, embracing the greater part of the land along the west side of the River Dart, was held by John Fleming Esq of Bigadon. The remainder of the parish was chiefly freehold and belonged to other owners. The Brook estate was sold by the Earl of Macclesfield in 1914.

The varied nature of the topography inevitably affected the life styles - and possibly the characters - of the people who lived in the different parts of the parish, and probably how they regarded going to church. For those in the town or at Buckfast it would be 'going up', whilst people dwelling at Scorriton, Combe, or Brook probably said they were 'going in'.

These variations of expression would also hint at the climatic differences of the parish's two extremes. Down in the valley areas weather may be reasonably temperate, but towards the upper levels conditions can be far more rigorous, with biting winds, fog, driving rain, and sometimes snow. In the past 'out awver' was regarded in the urbanised area with some awe, and crossing the moor seen as something of an adventure. Nevertheless, the nearer areas of moorland were often enjoyed in summer time by the lowlanders. Wallaford Down, before it was enclosed and fenced by its owner in 1939, was a favourite location for picnics, conveniently reached on foot from the town or by horse transport. There was no need to venture farther - fresh air and freedom were amply available there, and enjoyed by all.

See page 93 for notes on Chapter 1

2
⁂ THE TOWN OF BUCKFASTLEIGH ⁂

It is likely that a small community had already become settled in the valley of the River Mardle, possibly involved with wool processing and presenting a need, in the thirteenth century, for the church to be built on the hill above. By this time the abbey at Buckfast was well established and the abbot, holder of the manorial rights, would doubtless have been aware of the spiritual needs of the growing population, who would not have been permitted to worship in the abbey church itself. For this reason, and probably in order to retain the population's ties in his manor, he provided for construction of the parish church for the people.

There are various possible suggestions concerning the choice of situation. Perhaps in lifting his eyes to the hills the abbot decided that the high location, roughly equidistant from the growing inhabitation of Buckfast's 'leigh' area and from the dwellings clustered around the abbey precincts was the most fair, and convenient. Possibly the drier, elevated site was considered preferable to what was still mainly undrained, flood-vulnerable valley land.

Whilst Buckfast - its abbey and its inhabitants - benefited from the proximity of the River Dart, and from the Holy Brook bringing water from Holne Moor for living requirements and for industry, it has never developed into more than a village - latterly an adjunct of Buckfastleigh. (In 1994 Buckfast's population was just one sixth that of Buckfastleigh as a whole). Buckfastleigh, on the other hand, served by both the Mardle and the Dean Burn in their flow to join the Dart, grew to become a small town, as it has remained.

The medieval development of Buckfastleigh as a town can be traced through a study of its historic plan. This is made up of two distinct elements - Higher Town, centred around the market, and Lower Town, which had Fore Street as its main thoroughfare. The medieval origins of both 'Towns' are witnessed through the pattern of long narrow property boundaries running at right angles from Market and Fore Streets. Until the building of the chapels and other buildings along Chapel Street in the mid nineteenth century, Higher and Lower Towns were separated from each other by open land.

It is difficult to show which of the two Towns is the older settlement but there is some evidence to suggest the Higher Town, with its focus on the market, came first, while Lower Town was established as the woollen cloth industry expanded. In 1353 Buckfastleigh was granted a weekly market which was held for some centuries on Tuesdays, until the early 1800s.

The special qualities of Dartmoor water, its copious and swift flow, and its softness, besides providing power for the grinding of corn, were conducive to the particular industries that developed here - most importantly the processing of wool from the backs of sheep that grazed the moor and its foothills, and the tanning of skins for leather. Users also included - from the eighteenth century - a paper mill by the River Dart at Kilbury, and later an iron foundry in the town.

The working of wool had been long established in the area by the time of the Cistercians' arrival at Buckfast. Then, the abbots, who were members of the guilds, fostered and encouraged the woollen trade. The site of Higher Mill at Buckfast, served by Holy Brook water from Dartmoor, was probably that of the Cistercians' earlier mill building. Raw wool was a valuable trading commodity and many local people were

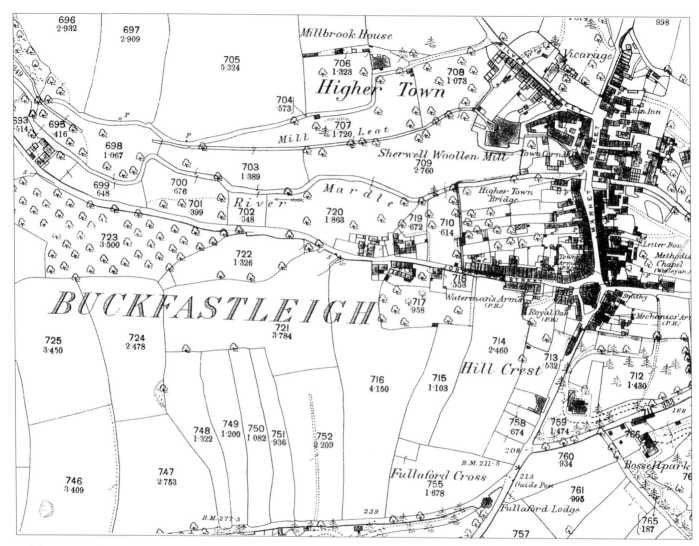

Higher Town from the Ordnance Survey map of the early twentieth century.

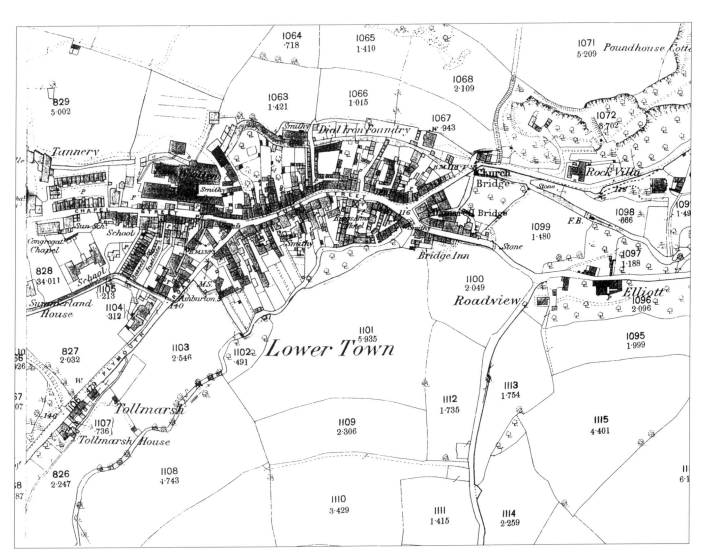

Lower Town from the Ordnance Survey map of the early twentieth century.

involved in wool-stapling, in some cases as a sideline or second source of income. Spinning and weaving of wool were done by people in their homes, with the unfinished cloth being taken to a fulling or tucking mill for final treatment.

Although, from the eighteenth century, Devon suffered a decline in its wool trade, here the industry survived, with the manufacture of serge for the Chinese market, sold through the East India Company, continuing until 1833. And after this date the parish's importance even continued to rise. In 1838 Buckfastleigh had 700 looms[1] - more than any other town in Devon and almost a quarter of those remaining in the county. Advances into mechanisation during the nineteenth century changed the character of the industry from being largely domestic or workshop based to becoming factory-centred. At Buckfast a worsted spinning frame was set up in 1817, and other mechanical equipment installed. The advent of wool-combing machines profoundly affected the lives of many people in the town. In 1850 eighteen master-combers were employing 300 people, but unwillingness or inability to advance to mechanisation put several of these masters out of business.[2]

One of the businesses that survived, at least for a time, was Churchwards'. Their mill stood on the Mardle's left bank immediately above the bridge in Market Street (the location also of the former Town corn mill). The building was destroyed by fire on 20 April 1906 but the chimney was left standing for some years. Another, which flourished well into the twentieth century, was Hamlyns', beside the Mardle in Chapel Street. This property, the Town Mill formerly called 'Sage's', was bought by Joseph Hamlyn in 1846. The Hamlyns were already established in the locality. In 1809 Joseph Hamlyn, who was of a farming family

The mill chimney stands in the ruins of Churchwards' woollen mill following the fire of 20 April 1906.

from South Brent, in partnership with Benjamin Hayman, had bought a tannery at Buckfastleigh, close to the Mardle in Higher Town, and used it for fellmongery and later for the hand-combing of wool from the sheepskins bought for tanning.

In 1818 Hayman left the partnership, but Hamlyn was later joined by his three sons, Joseph, John and William. In 1842 they rented premises at West Mill for the combing until they installed machinery for the purpose at the Town Mill, where cloth manufacture, using locally collected wools, became the main production. At around the same time the Hamlyns also purchased and similarly used the Higher Mill at Buckfast.[3]

An early twentieth century view of Hamlyn's Mill at Buckfastleigh.

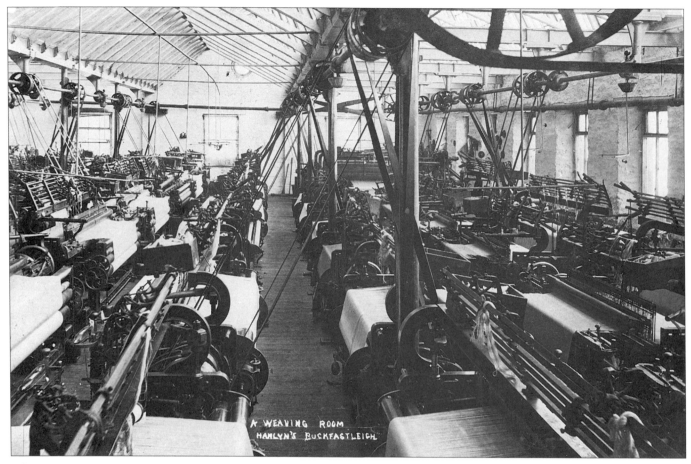

A WEAVING ROOM
HAMLYN'S BUCKFASTLEIGH

The weaving room at Hamlyn's Mill.

Also at Buckfast, and closer to the Dart, was the large mill of John Berry and Company, sergemakers and woolcombers, and makers of blankets, who moved here from Ashburton in 1850. The large workforce became unemployed when, on the night of Monday 19 November 1877, Berry's Mill was destroyed by fire, which originated in the wheeling shed.[4] Rebuilding quickly followed and the rows of blankets hanging out to dry in the field beside the Dart again became a familiar sight.

In 1920 Hamlyns sold their Buckfastleigh business to the Co-operative Wholesale Society, and woollen manufacture continued under the CWS. During these years 'the mill' was the workplace for very many Buckfastleigh people, who developed skills that covered the range of those required in textile manufacture. The 'hooter' was a familiar sound punctuating the working day. Although in earlier times the hours of work were 6am to 6pm, later the hooter would be heard at 7.55am, 12 noon, 1.25 or 1.30pm, and 6pm. With the quarries and Buckfast Mill also having similar sounds the local air could at times be almost melodious. By 1973, however, the industry had declined, the mill was closed, and demolition of much of the factory structure followed, including the tall chimney stack. The remaining premises, purchased by Teignbridge District Council, are now used by various smaller enterprises, with fellmongery (the curing of skins) continuing on the site. At Buckfast, where in 1979 the mill beside the Dart also lost its chimney stack, the Buckfast Spinning Company maintains the local link with woollen manufacturing in the spinning of yarn for carpets.

Not surprisingly, with thriving industry, the population of Buckfastleigh increased during the nineteenth century.[5] From a figure of 1,525 in 1801 the number rose to 2,613 in 1851 and to a peak of 2,781 in 1901, followed by a fall to 2,410 in 1931. In the 1990s the population of Buckfastleigh is a little over 2,000. With a shorter life expectancy in the 1800s the average ages would have been lower than today, with a higher proportion of younger people and children in the community. Disease, however, was always a fearful enemy to be reckoned with. Tuberculosis, or consumption as it was then known, took a dreadful toll on many lives. Diphtheria was another disease that could decimate families. During August 1856 my Warren great-grandparents, John and Rebecca, who lived in Fore Street, lost from diphtheria all three of the small children they then had, aged respectively six, four, and two (all are buried in Buckfastleigh churchyard) - just a month before the first of their later children was born.[6] Infection was a great concern, and sometimes called for stern measures to be taken. Around 1860 my maternal great-great-grandfather, Owen McKiernan, surgeon in

Buckfastleigh, returned to his home, Rockfield, by the Mardle, after sitting at night with a friend (believed to have been the vicar of Dean Prior) as he died from smallpox. He would not enter the house until the copper had been lit and water heated for his bath, and all his clothes plus his riding saddle were burnt in the copper's fire.[7] Scarlet fever was at times also epidemic.

Life and activity, however, generally pervaded the town and the people were generally law-abiding, and unexceptional. The vicar Robert Bradford, when he reported to Dean Milles in the 1750s, wrote that the inhabitants were 'For the most part very industrious and frugal in their diet'. Nevertheless, they probably had their fling at the times of the fairs, for cattle, sheep and horses, and for wool, held in June and September. The fairs took place at the foot of Church Hill, at Sun Cross and lasted for three days. Farmers from all around would attend, and the sheep were arranged for selling against the then Vicarage wall, and along Market (now Church) Street.[8]

It is interesting to compare this view of the bridge over the Mardle with that of Stockdale's drawing shown overleaf. The Sun Inn can be seen; cars have replaced the sheep!

A drawing of 1854 by F.W.L. Stockdale showing the bridge across the Mardle at the bottom of Market Street. This view looks along Bridge Street towards the Sun Inn and shows some of the traditional town buildings that have since been demolished. (Reproduced by kind permission of the Royal Institution of Cornwall and with the help of Dr Todd Gray.).

Although Buckfastleigh had originally been granted its fair in 1461,[9] when it was held from 24-26 August - on the feast of St Bartholomew - later this was preceded by an additional one, held to coincide with the feast of St Peter on the third Thursday in June,[10] which may have carried the tradition of the eating of lambs'-tail pies. These were still the customary fair dates at the time of the Milles questionnaire but at least by 1850 the August fair had been moved to the second Thursday in September, when pear-pies were the accustomed delicacy. These would be prepared on the previous day, and on the blowing of a horn at 8 o'clock in the evening people without ovens would take their pies to the Sun Inn to be baked overnight, ready for the next morning. For the occasion a large swing, capable of holding ten adults or a greater number of children, called a 'goozing boat', would be set up near the Town Mill. Before the proceedings began the children would have to sing:[11]

Buckfastleigh Fair is here again
With pretty young maids and bright young men,
Some come in from Wallaford Down,
Some come in from Widecombe Town.

Then they would call out: 'Swing us up higher Mr Mugford,' and, as the ropes were pulled, up would go the swing. The cost per person was one penny. These fairs continued at least to the later years of the nineteenth century, long after the weekly markets had ceased to operate. However, an occasional cattle fair, or auction, and sometimes a funfair, used to be held up to the First World War in a field in the town called Glover's Park, before houses were built there.

Around the middle of the nineteenth century there were no fewer than sixteen public houses in Buckfastleigh. These comprised:- the Sun Inn; the Town Arms and Waterman's Arms in Market Street; the Mechanics' on Crest Hill; the Royal Oak in Jordan Street; the Golden Lion above Weech Corner and the Bell and the Globe below; the Prince of Wales and the White Hart in Plymouth Road; the King's Arms, Commercial Arms, and Valiant Soldier in Fore Street; the Bridge Inn at Elliott Plain, and the Half Moon along the road towards Dean. There was also the Coffee Tavern in Chapel Street. Cider was the popular drink, made in large quantities from apples grown in the local area - in one year an orchard of one acre produced 4,000 gallons.[12]

Early postcard view of Bridge Street looking towards Market Street.

Whether due to the cider drinking or not, it was sometimes necessary for wrongdoers to be taken into custody, and for this purpose there was a lock-up, or clink, sited opposite the present 'Co-op' shop in Chapel Street. On the other hand, stray animals could be secured in the Pound, located on Crest or Cock Hill, where a gate led to a small yard and outhouse near the meeting of the two ascending roads. Farmers had to pay a fine of one shilling in order to reclaim them.[13]

The growth of nonconformity led to the establishment of particular places of worship within the town.[14] Independent worship was brought to Buckfastleigh in the eighteenth century by the Revd Richard Bickle who was given leave to use the market house which then stood in the centre of Market Street. After Bickle's death there followed a spell without a minister, but in 1798 a tenement building, standing on waste ground in what became known as Chapel Street, was purchased from a local serge maker for £90 for use by the Independents, and was called 'Chapel House'. This was later demolished and in 1875 the newly built Congregational Church was opened on the site. (This church building eventually became redundant and part of it, re-named the Loosemore Centre, is now used by an organ builder). On the opposite side of Chapel Street an impressive Wesleyan Chapel was built in 1835 to replace two earlier chapel buildings farther down the street, which have been demolished. The 1835 construction, the Methodist Church, is now the place of worship of both the Methodists and the United Reformed Church (embodying the former Congregationalists). Next to it is the Roman Catholic Parish Church of St Benedict, built in 1939. Another group of worshippers, known as the Christian Community, meet at the former Young Men's Christian Association building, opposite St Benedict's. There is also a small Methodist Church at Buckfast, built in 1891, and another at Scorriton.

Buckfastleigh's increasing population and developments of the time caused concern to be felt by various people during the nineteenth century regarding the education - or its non-existence - for the children. There seems to have been a reluctance to provide any schooling until well into the 1800s, partly due to a lack of initiative by the clergy (perhaps because half of the tithe was appropriated by lay rectors elsewhere) and also because of the demand for child labour by the local industries.[15] In the eighteenth century there were only private dame schools in the town,[16] and when completing a parliamentary return in 1818,[17] the then vicar reported that there were three schools with a total of eighty children, all private and fee-paying. There was no interest in educating poorer members of the community. By 1833[18] there were eight paying schools with a reported total of 131 boy pupils and 125 girls. There was also a free Wesleyan Sunday School of 80 boys and 150 girls and a Calvinist Sunday School claiming to have 30 boys and 30 girls. When the Wesleyan Chapel was built in 1835 a British (mainly nonconformist) day school was established in a room underneath it at a total cost of £356.14s.

There was no Church of England school - Sunday or otherwise - and this was a matter of discomfiture to the vicar, the Revd Matthew Lowndes, B.A. The problem was particularly acute as, in the mid 1830s, Buckfastleigh was suffering a spell of depression. Although the town was to survive the decline of the wool trade that affected Devon in general in the nineteenth century, competition from Yorkshire's mills and the ending of the East India Company's monopoly were having their effects, and at this time Hamlyns' mill was not yet established. On 20 April 1837 Mr Lowndes completed a return to the Diocese of Exeter, relating to education.[19] From his rather faded handwritten report it is possible to gain something of an impression of Buckfastleigh at that period. He wrote of the 'intense distress prevailing among a dense manufacturing population' which was 'at present wholly unemployed', of the 'general poverty of the parishioners' and the 'deplorable fact that no school exists among us which can claim to be a Church of England school'. The report continued:

Our church is situated on the top of a steep hill, rather more than half a mile from our large village and consequently repeated attempts to take the children to church on Sunday have failed, every winter or continuation of bad weather undoing what we have been labouring to effect at other times. Since 1813, during the incumbency of my Father, I succeeded in setting on foot a school for the children of the poor and we opened with 200 the first morning. It was conducted in such a manner as to stimulate a neighbouring large town, Totnes, and several adjoining parishes, to adopt a similar course ...

I continued to support the school almost wholly for many years, until I found that the burden when thrown on my shoulders accordingly was becoming too oppressive and then there was not the co-opera-

tion which the peculiarity of the circumstances, under which I was placed, seemed to require. Every feeling of that sort, however, I have long since thrown aside, and I am now most anxious that the children of my poorer parishioners should have the means of being educated in the principles of the church. I have no longer the means of contributing to such an object in the way I could wish, and we have scarcely any resident proprietors. Our manufactories are filled with dissenters and most of our tradesmen are of the same description. From them every effort on my part to keep up a school meets with a strong undercurrent of opposition.

Although I have met with so many discouragements I am not disheartened, yet I still think that the distance of the church from the village where there is a large Wesleyan as well as a Calvinistic meeting house is an altogether insurmountable obstacle - The titles of my living, although the parish is so large (in consequence of the best part of the parish being Abbey land) seldom reach to £150 a year, and a sense of justice to my family prevents my embarking on any scheme of building this church on a spot near the village without security against such a responsibility in such as would be attended with hazard. Besides there are no grounds for expecting assistance in such an undertaking from any public body without our raising large local contributions and the fact is that we could raise among ourselves, nothing. We have the greatest difficulty in keeping up even a child-bed linen charity, the subscriptions to which are barely seven pounds a year, though our population borders on 3,000, mainly the manufacturing and agricultural labourers... Our Poor Rate is an intolerable burden and indeed so general is the distress to be seen in every direction around us that I never dream of making an attempt to raise a collection for any public purpose.

The report was apparently received with due attention at the diocesan office, with the appropriate committee being prepared to assist with funds towards providing a schoolroom 'in the heart of the village' subject to the bishop's recommendation. The extent of such eventual contribution is not known, but steps towards the provision of a National (Church) School proceeded over the next few years with funds being raised locally.

My maternal great-great-grandmother, Helena Louisa Worrall, was one who helped with the finding of money for the school. Miss Worrall, following the

Helena Louisa Worrall, the author's great-great grandmother, who helped to raise money for the National School. Here she is portrayed in her riding attire, doubtless that which she wore when out collecting subscriptions. Taken from an early silhouette photograph of c. 1842.

deaths of her parents, had come to Buckfastleigh from London to take up residence as a lodger in the vicarage in the late 1820s or early 1830s. Exactly why she came to this particular place is not clear, but she is known to have been delicate in health and probably the Devon air was considered desirable. And such an arrangement was probably the result of some seeking, or recommendation, as far as the vicar, the Revd Matthew Lowndes, was concerned, in view of his admitted impecunious circumstances and the fact that there would have been rooms to spare in the large vicarage. (Although the earlier, smaller, vicarage had been at the far end of Jordan Street, at Sainthill opposite the then tithe barn,[20] a new vicarage had been built in the late eighteenth century on the north side of Silver Street, approached by a drive from what is now Church Street).[21]

Helen Worrall was not without means, and she apparently arrived at the vicarage in some style. According to family belief, she brought with her a maid, groom, and two riding horses, along with her own silverware, and she paid the vicar £100 per year for herself, and £100 for her maid, groom, and horses. She was firmly christian, highly educated, reputedly could speak five languages, was skilled at needlework, and she used to have some of the poorer girls from Buckfastleigh to her sitting room and teach them to sew, read and write.

Undoubtedly, from her observations and through living at the vicarage, she would have become well aware of the local needs, and she undertook the collecting of money to finance the establishment of a National School. From information passed down to me I understand that she rode out on her horse to collect contributions from well-to-do people, and apparently herself provided half the necessary sum. (In 1842 Helen married the local doctor, Irishman Owen McKiernan, at Holy Trinity Church. She died in 1857, aged forty-four or forty-five, and is buried in Buckfastleigh churchyard. The McKiernans' eldest child, Clare, married William Furneaux and they lived at Rose Cottage in Silver Street until they died, in 1912 and 1910 respectively. They were my great-grandparents).

Gradually the necessary money was raised and with the help of a government grant of £189 the National School was built in Chapel Street, and came into being in 1841-2. In 1848 it had 7 boys and 76 girls on its books, with average attendances respectively 48 and 46. £20 income came from subscriptions and £20 from fees ('school pence'), and expenditure was £40 in salaries and £1.14s elsewhere - the deficit probably being met by the vicar.

In 1847 the school was listed as one of those 'not in a satisfactory state and in need of great alterations to become satisfactory,' and 'discipline very deficient, method unsatisfactory, instruction very little in either school' (this probably includes the neighbouring British School) 'and what is learnt is only by rote. Master not mild and gentle enough, mistress quite inefficient'.[22] The master and mistress, who may have been a local husband and wife, were untrained and unqualified. Efforts towards improvement were later made with the aid of grants and the appointment of certificated teachers - Henry Berry in 1859 and William I. Parsons in 1860. In 1862 there were two certificated teachers (for boys and for girls) and two pupil-teachers. However, the Revised Code of 1862, which ended state payment of pupil-teachers and augmentation of certificated teachers' salaries, brought disaster. The trained teachers and pupil-teachers were dismissed and untrained ones appointed. This arrangement continued until the establishment of the School Board in 1871, with the existing schools remaining in use until the Board School was opened in 1875 but with expenses met by school rate.

The British School had also been struggling. The enquiry following the 1870 Act found, for the two schools:

National School - accommodation 240, present 63 boys, 35 girls.

British School - accommodation 192, present 48 boys, 38 girls.

Thus, not nearly as many Buckfastleigh children were regularly attending school in the 1870s as should have been. There was clearly a pressing need for the School Board.

And so, the present school, now Buckfastleigh Primary, became established on its present site in 1875. In 1936, and more recently, it has been enlarged and modernised, and has benefited from a succession of dedicated teachers. One of them was my aunt, Marjorie Mary Warren, who was on the staff for twenty-seven years - latterly as Deputy Head - before her retirement in 1959.

The former National School building still stands in Chapel Street, next to the Co-op shops. Over the years it has served a variety of purposes, including for Sunday School, for temporary day school use during alterations to the newer one, for Sunday evening services before the provision in 1894 of St Luke's Church, as a Civic Restaurant from 1948-50 (when a kitchen was added), and for Girl Guide, Women's Institute and other meetings. It is now a youth centre.

At Buckfast, St Mary's Convent School, for boys and girls, was established by nuns in 1901 in a building dating from 1893. Although it was a Roman Catholic school with lay teachers, children of other denominations were taken. The convent closed in 1987 but the school continued as St Mary's Primary. In 1894 a Church of England Board School was built at Buckfast. It closed as a school in 1920, but the building continued in use for another purpose, as the Violet Evelyn Institute (see Chapter three).

The former National School building in Chapel Street.

Located as it is, midway between Exeter and Plymouth, Buckfastleigh was undoubtedly influenced in its growth by being on the direct route, and transport systems have evolved and changed through the centuries. In early days roads - such as existed - were narrow, steep, undulating and badly surfaced. Improvements came with developments of the Turnpike Trusts in the late eighteenth century, and were furthered in the early nineteenth century following a report by the County Bridge Surveyor, James Green.

One of his recommendations was the widening of the fourteenth century Dart Bridge[23], just east of Buckfastleigh, on the Exeter-Plymouth turnpike, and this was done in 1827. In 1929 this bridge was reconstructed and further widened. Early travellers from the east crossed the river here and then had a choice of routes. A very ancient track to the west ascended Church Hill from Dart Bridge by a steep narrow lane known as Fairies' Hall, and this continued close to the church. The route for the town proceeded around the foot of the hill, heading for the River Mardle, which it

Dart Bridge looking towards the old tollhouse which was demolished when the A38 road was modernised.

Church (or Harps) Bridge, over the Mardle.

An early photograph of Church Steps which people still climb on their way to Holy Trinity Church from the town.

DAMERELL'S BRIDGE 1912
BUCKFASTLEIGH, BEFORE RE-BUILDING

Damerell's (or Barter's) Bridge at the lower end of Fore Street. Setter's Bridge Inn is seen in the background and the author's grandfather, John Warren, stands in a white apron on the bridge. The photograph is dated 1912.

crossed by Church (formerly Harps) Bridge. Walking access to the church was provided from near the bridge, by the ascent of the 196 Church Steps - constructed in the nineteenth century, or earlier, and listed now as being of special historic or architectural interest (they were repaired in 1982). Traffic leaving the town for Totnes would cross the Dean Burn in Lower Town by Damarell's or Barter's Bridge, cross Elliott Plain and proceed along what is now called Old Totnes Road to Austin's Bridge over the Dart. Possibly of medieval origin, this former packhorse bridge must have had much wool, and also mining products, carried over it, bound for the ports of Totnes and Dartmouth. Forms of transport continuing to Plymouth would proceed through the town - perhaps breaking the journey at one or other of the inns -

Austin's Bridge over the River Dart on the old route to Totnes.

branching left at Weech Corner towards Dean Prior, while those heading for the moor or the church would bear right at this corner, continue through Higher Town, and across the Mardle again - by ford or wooden footbridge before the bridge was constructed in the mid nineteenth century. Then came the steep hill, with the moor lying away to the left, the church to the right. The improvement of the main roads made possible the regular running of horse-drawn coaches by the 1820s. Speed became competitive and in 1835 the Devonport Mail coach *Quicksilver* reached Devonport from London in just over 21 hours.[24] One can imagine the noise and clatter these regular services would make as they advanced up Buckfastleigh's Fore Street, and the hustle and bustle of a necessary stop and probably change of horses.

A major improvement to the road system came in 1927, when the town's first by-pass road was constructed across Elliott Plain and along the southern fringe of the town. The work necessitated the diversion of the Dean Burn, the building of two bridges, and cutting through the steep slopes of the hill. The road was named Strode Road, after the chairman of Devon County Council's Reconstruction Committee. In the early 1970s this road was itself by-passed by the construction of the A38 dual carriageway road, completed from Exeter to Plymouth in 1974. The Buckfastleigh section includes the Mardle viaduct, which in 1974 won a national award for excellence in the use of steel.[25] Plans are afoot for yet another relief road on the north side of Church Hill, cutting through Buckfast, to facilitate passage of heavy vehicles servicing the industrial area of the former Town Mill.

The railway came to Buckfastleigh in the form of a branch of the South Devon Railway, from Totnes to Ashburton. Its opening, on 1 May 1872, was accompanied by great celebrations in the field near the station. My grandfather, John William Warren, then at boarding school in Newton Abbot, and his friend Eddie Churchward (later of Hillside), were given special permission to come home for the occasion, and they rode on the inaugural journey. My grandmother, (later his wife), then Harriette Alice Hoare, as a young girl also attended the event. It was a very warm day and she always remembered how the white stockings she was wearing stuck to her legs in the heat. The railway fulfilled a busy life, notably in carrying goods from and for the woollen mills. Coal was carried in huge quantities and the shunting of scores of trucks, many of them bearing Welsh names strange to a child's eyes, was a daily spectacle. Also of course the railway, which became part of the Great Western, provided comfortable transport for passengers, either to nearby towns or to link into the main network. Sadly, in 1958, a few years after nationalisation, the railway was closed, but it was subsequently bought by the Dart Valley Light Railway Company, under which it became developed as a popular tourist attraction. It now operates as the South Devon Railway.

Reference to Kelly's Directory of 1850 (see Appendix 7) will show the numerous trades existing in

Early photograph of Fore Street before the days of motorised traffic.

Buckfastleigh a century and a half ago that have now vanished from the scene. But many of the names of families and individuals are the same, as established 'Buckfastleighites' will recognise. Many such names also crop up repeatedly in the church registers from the seventeenth century. In some cases there is variation of spelling, but this is due to the way the spoken name was heard and written down by the clerk, or parson, and means little. My own family name, Warren, is an example, variously spelt as Warring, Warringe, Warrin and eventually standardised as Warren. The Buckfastleigh Parish Register shows that a John Warringe was churchwarden in 1641-2, and in 1674 a Daniel Warren had 5 hearths. (The average number of hearths per household in Devon at that time, as calculated by Stoate, was 2.0).[26] The family was involved in the woollen business for generations, particularly in woolcombing, but were overtaken by incoming mechanisation in the mid nineteenth century. My great-grandfather John Warren diversified into saddlery, and his son - my grandfather - followed him as a saddler, a trade which he pursued together with other business interests until he retired in the early 1930s. He was much involved in local affairs in Buckfastleigh, and, like his early forbear, a churchwarden - for twenty-one years until he died at the age of eighty in 1940.

Architecturally the town of Buckfastleigh cannot be regarded as displaying a high degree of grandeur or noteworthy style. Nevertheless, it has numerous urban buildings of historic and vernacular interest, many of which, in a survey of 1993, were officially identified as listed buildings. Of particular note is the town's rare and important surviving pattern of back 'courts'. Often approached from the street by an 'ope', the courts were usually formed behind owners' dwellings where there was access to river or brook, space for buildings used for woolcombing and other industrial processes, with workers' cottages.

Work involving cloth was also carried on in people's homes, such as in those known as Weavers Cottages, listed as Grade II* historic buildings, in Chapel Street. In these houses the upper storey formed a tentering loft where wet cloth was hung up by the selvedges and stretched on tenterhooks to dry in the through current of air generated by opening the louvres on the walls. There were numerous such tentering places in Buckfastleigh. There are, however, no gracious houses sited along the main street such as are seen, for example, in Ashburton. When the Hamlyns held their influence in the town they provided houses for the workers near the mill, but their own mansions were sited out on the fringe. Fullaford, Bossell, Hapstead, and Cleavehurst were all built by members of the Hamlyn family.[27] A public building that is worthy of note is the Town Hall in Bossell Road. Given by the Hamlyns, it was constructed 1887-8 of local lime-stone faced with Bath stone and brick, and was extended in 1925. (A board showing the old market and fair tolls is now displayed in its foyer). Another is St Luke's Church, built in 1894. (This currently serves as the parish church, and is the subject of a separate publication by this author).[28] The nearby Victoria Park and the open-air swimming pool were provided for the town in 1897 to mark Queen Victoria's Diamond Jubilee.

Dwellings in the town mostly had wells which in earlier days provided 'drinking' water. But this was vulnerable to pollution and in 1892 caused a serious typhoid epidemic.[29] Water was then piped from a spring near the town to a series of taps from which households fetched their supplies, until piping to individual houses became general. The town's water was then piped in from a catchment area at Lambsdown,[30] near Wallaford, with collecting chamber and 250,000 gallon reservoir, until in the mid twentieth century the responsibility for supplies came under the main water authority. A sewage disposal works was established in the last years of the nineteenth century in fields on the right bank of the Dart, below the town. After the Second World War the system was improved, with provision of a modern works at Kilbury.

A gasworks was pioneered at Buckfast in 1868, but evidently with limitations. Later, with prospects enhanced by the opening of the railway to Buckfastleigh and easier availability of coal supplies, attempts were made to form a gas company, and eventually, in 1898 the Buckfastleigh Gas Company was formed.[31] In 1912 this firm became part of Devon Gas Association Ltd, which continued to serve the neighbourhood until nationalisation in 1949, when it was taken over by the South Western Gas Board. Subsequently the Buckfast gasometer was used only for storage of gas piped here until that familiar feature was removed in the 1980s. Buckfastleigh's first electricity supply station was in the former West Mill (near the Plymouth Road west of the town, by Whitecleaves Quarry). Trial work began here around 1904 when the old wooden water-wheel which, powered by water from the Dean Burn led in by a leat and launder, had formerly been used for grinding corn, was converted for generating electricity. The new demands put an increased strain on the old wheel, and although efforts were made to prolong its life by driving in iron wedges, it was removed in 1907 and replaced with a turbine. This continued in use for some years in conjunction with a producer gas engine.[32]

During the twentieth century, particularly between, and since, the two world wars, Buckfastleigh and Buckfast have seen many new housing developments as people sought more space and modern living conditions. With smaller families, and more people living alone and for longer, the proportion of homes in relation to population has risen. There are no longer the numerous large families, with several members employed locally - such as 'in the mill' - and all living in one house. Descendants of many of those earlier families are now dispersed in homes with gardens in a range of locations. Over the years their numbers have been joined by incomers - retired people, and others who may commute daily to work in the bigger towns - and in many cases these have brought new life to former workers' cottages, which have been updated to stylish 'mews' residences, at greatly enhanced values. A look through some of the opes at well-kept flower-adorned courts can give an indication of the transformation.

See page 94 for notes on Chapter 2.

3
⚜ BUCKFAST ABBEY ⚜

As has already been said (see page 10) Buckfast predates the town of Buckfastleigh, having developed from the establishment of the first Benedictine abbey here in the year 1018. It was one of several monasteries founded by King Canute who saw the value to the country of their stabilising influence. The name of the first abbot is not known, but the Domesday Book identifies the holder of that office in 1066 as Alwin. The abbey lands in 1086 comprised the 300 acres of the manor of Buckfast ('Bulfestr') with which it had been endowed, and also nearly 10,000 acres of several other manors in different parts of Devon, from which it received income.[1]

After half a century of decline following Domesday, new life was introduced around 1136 with the arrival from Normandy of Savignac monks. In 1147 they were consolidated into the Cistercian order, which continued the occupancy of Buckfast until the Dissolution in 1539. Under the Cistercians life at the abbey was plain and demanding. The Rule was that of St Benedict, but in its more austere aspect. Divine Office comprised six daily services totalling six hours - the first observance being that of matins at 2 a.m. - in a setting devoid of embellishment or ornamentation. Diet was plain and simple, habits were of crude woollen fabric worn next to the skin, and there were no luxuries and no leisure. Prayer and work were the main activities of the monks' ascetic existence.

The Cistercian Order was in its ascendancy during the twelfth century, and was itself a contributory factor towards great advances in Europe and beyond at this time. Agriculture was one way in which a lead was given, in the improvement of pasture land and of sheep farming, with the Cistercians becoming major producers in England's increasingly prosperous wool trade. At this time vigorous building work was in progress at Buckfast. The early abbey was probably constructed mainly of wood, and this was replaced by the Cistercians with buildings of stone, on a more extensive scale. Although little of their above-ground structure has survived into modern times (just the north gate arch and part of the barrel-vaulted undercroft and other fragments are still to be seen), archaeological excavations in the 1980s indicate the extent of the Cistercians' buildings and general layout.[2]

Money problems caused by demands on the abbey's income from wool for financing the Crusades, and the levy of huge sums by King John, following his quarrels with the Pope and excommunication in 1209, made life extremely difficult for the abbot and his community. But the abbey struggled to survive, and the outlook revived as the thirteenth century advanced, manifested in further building work and increased influence in the wider community. Wool exports were booming - particularly to Italy - although it was observed that the quality of Buckfast wool was lower than that from Forde Abbey (near Chard) apparently because of the sheep being grazed on Dartmoor. Corn was also produced, evidenced by the existence of a grange barn at Buckfast, and on Dean Moor remains of obviously pastoral farming, including a steading and byre, were excavated by Lady Aileen Fox in 1956 before being submerged beneath the Avon Reservoir.[3] At the end of the century Buckfast Abbey received a visit from King Edward I, from 8-10 April 1297.

Fish formed an important part of the diet of the abbey community, readily supplied by the adjacent River Dart under rights that were firmly guarded.

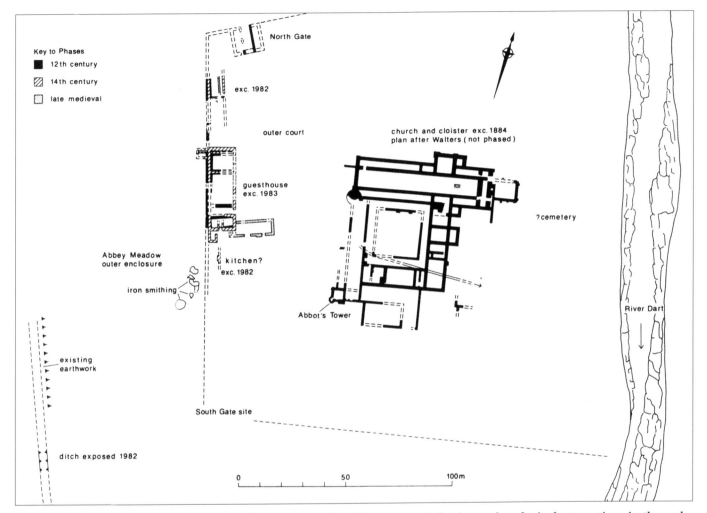

Plan showing the known extent of the medieval layout of Buckfast Abbey, following archaeological excavations in the early 1980s. (Reproduced by permission of Stewart Brown and the Devon Archaeological Society.).

Buckfast Abbey shared in the scourge of the Black Death in the mid fourteenth century, with two of its abbots and several monks dying apparently from the terrible disease. The population was decimated, income declined and some of the abbey buildings fell into disuse and decay. However, fortunes again revived, and by the fifteenth century Buckfast owned much wealth, and at the same time was fulfilling its responsibilities to the parish and those in need, and in the advancement of learning. Mostly the life-elected abbots were dedicated and respected, but in the early part of the fifteenth century Abbot William Beaghe's unsatisfactory government and administration of the abbey in spiritual and temporal matters was causing loss of confidence and discord in the community, and eventually accusations of his immorality were revealed. The situation was restored by his resignation in 1432.

The Hundred Years' War caused difficulties of travel on the Continent, and particularly inhibited visits by the Cistercians to the mother house at Cîteaux. At the same time hospitality was dispensed at the abbey to travellers, as was the Benedictine custom, and this increased as the fifteenth century advanced with varying standards being provided according to the status of the visitor. The remains of the medieval guest house can still be seen today.

By the sixteenth century there was a decline in the monastic population throughout the country, the number of monks and nuns having fallen from around 20,000 in the thirteenth century to 12,000 in 1500. But their property had not been significantly reduced, and about a quarter of the country was in monastic ownership, producing a comfortable revenue of which only a small proportion was being used for charitable purposes. In some cases the monasteries' work had been superseded by growing universities and other institutions, and a number had already closed.

In 1535 a detailed survey of church property was made on behalf of King Henry VIII, who appointed Thomas Cromwell to carry out a reform. Cromwell had already dealt with incidences of rebellion against the king with rigorous severity, and in view of his reputation he and his commissioners faced no great opposition. In fact, communities in general were remarkably compliant, force was rarely necessary, and reasonable terms were arranged, including generous pensions to abbots and monks who co-operated.

At Buckfast, however, there seem to have been an element of intrigue. In 1535 a new abbot, Gabriel Donne, had been imposed upon the abbey. Donne was related by marriage to Thomas Cromwell and had recently been instrumental in deceptively bringing the informer, and opponent of the king, Thomas Tyndale from exile in Flanders back to England and to execution. The Buckfast appointment was apparently his reward, and one that put him into a position of 'easing through' the process of Dissolution.

The actual day on which the Dissolution took effect at Buckfast was 25 February 1539, when the commissioners, led by William Petre, brought the Deed of Surrender and witnessed its signing. Pensions were then assigned to the monks and the possessions of the abbey received. Some of the manors, previously owned by the abbey, which had now become the property of the king, were subsequently sold. The manor of Buckfast, including the abbey, was initially rented by Sir Thomas Dennys, who had held the important post of chief steward of the abbey, and subsequently bought by him in 1540. Dennys later married the sister of Gabriel Donne, and the manor remained in his family for 250 years. Dismantling and demolition of the buildings followed, although a few of the outer buildings were left and put to other uses. Among them the former guest house was converted to comprise various components which became Abbey Farm. The five bells of the abbey were reputedly bought by the parishioners of Buckfastleigh for £33.15s.

After the destructive activities of the Dissolution Buckfast sank into a state of comparative somnolence until around 1800. Although much of the abbey structure had been removed, many parts of the former buildings defied the elements and remained standing, including the north and south gates and the abbot's

Samuel Buck (1697-1779) print showing extensive ruins of the medieval abbey at Buckfast still standing. (Devon Books).

tower. Undoubtedly, easily recoverable stone was taken and utilised in the construction of other local buildings. Further clearance was made in the early years of the nineteenth century when local mill owner Samuel Berry bought the remaining walls, moved away unwanted rubble and constructed a neo-Gothic mansion on the site. The imposing building, which incorporated some of the abbey's features, was completed in 1806. By the 1840s Buckfast had become very much alive with industry, particularly of wool. As has been said, Higher Buckfast Mill was bought and worked by the Hamlyns, and Lower Mill by John Berry & Company for the making of serge and blankets.

The mansion built by Samuel Berry was sold by him following his bankruptcy in 1825, and was then owned by the Benthall family until 1872, when it was bought by Dr James Gale. In 1892 Dr Gale decided to sell, hoping that the property might again become a monastery. As a result it was leased, and later purchased by a religious community of Benedictine monks, who had been evicted from France because their particular branch of the Order was considered unauthorised.

And so, in October 1882, after nearly three and a half centuries, monks were again installed at Buckfast. Plans were soon afoot to restore the abbey, and public support was sought, and generously given. A committee was formed, including several eminent Roman Catholics, and the architect Frederick A Walters appointed. As work commenced the foundations of the original abbey became apparent, and these were used as basis for rebuilding. In 1899 Buckfast was given independent status and in 1902 again became an abbey, dedicated to St Mary. The first elected abbot was Boniface Natter, a noted scholar. Tragically, however, after less than four years in office, in 1906 Abbot Boniface was drowned in a shipwreck while on a voyage to the Argentine. Travelling with him was Dom Ascar Vonier, who survived the event and was subsequently elected as Buckfast's next abbot.

On 5 January 1907 the new abbot laid the foundation of the abbey church on the medieval foundations of its predecessor. Rebuilding gradually proceeded, as limited incoming funds permitted, with the monks themselves - usually a team of just four or six - carrying out the main part of the work. The progress was slow, but steady, enhanced by various gifts including fourteen bells. In 1922 the abbey church - as yet unfinished - was inaugurated and opened for worship. Work then advanced towards final completion, finance always being a limiting factor. Resources were aided, however, by the monastic enterprise of making and selling Buckfast's own brand 'Tonic Wine', and also by the increasing number of visitors who came here during the 1920s and '30s.

By 25 August 1932 the work was sufficiently complete for the Abbey Church to be consecrated, in what proved to be a great occasion.[4] The consecration was performed by the Papal Legate, Cardinal Bourne, and the ceremony was attended by eminent leading figures of the Roman Catholic Church and by crowds of people, many of whom could not be accommodated within the building but heard the service from loudspeakers placed outside. The event was widely reported in

This photograph of Buckfast predates 1905. The mill buildings and chimney dominate the scene as the rebuilding of the Abbey had yet to make an impact.

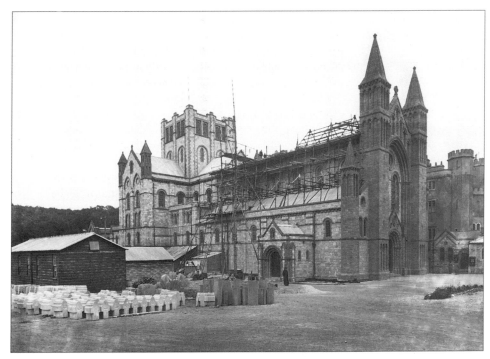

Two views of Buckfast Abbey show-ing the rebuilding of the abbey church at an advanced stage. The photograph on the left is reproduced by permission of the Royal Comm-ission on Historical Monuments of England. (Crown © reserved.). The lower picture is dated 3 September 1930.

Buckfast Abbey Church.

the national press as well as in the local papers. The *Totnes Times* covered nearly two pages of broadsheet with a detailed account of the occasion, of the personalities involved, and of the abbey's history.

The Abbey Church was still, however, without its full erected tower, and so had no means of hanging its bells. The tower was subsequently completed, the topping stone was laid in July 1937, and the final pointing finished at the end of 1938. Within just three weeks of the completion the much loved Abbot Ascar Vonier died. During the thirty-two years of his office Abbot Ascar had inspired the rebuilding and had lived, as he wished, to see its fulfilment. He was buried in the church's sanctuary.

The life of the Abbey and its relationship with the local community has developed under succeeding abbots. Bruno Fehrenbacher was abbot during the Second World War, when monks took part in the war effort in various ways, and in the immediate post-war years when the Abbey Church was further beautified with mosaic flooring and stained glass, and bee-keeping and breeding were developed to a high degree of speciality by one of the monks, Brother Adam Kehrle. The next abbot, from 1957 to 1976, was Dom Placid Hooper, Buckfast's first English abbot, under whom the Abbey's boys' preparatory school was opened in 1967, to survive until 1994. Amongst many changes during this period were ones concerning the Liturgy and the greater use of English, and certain modifications of the regime. Abbot Leo Smith followed, from 1976 to 1992, and during his time measures were taken to cater for the many visitors to the Abbey, with various external developments including car parks, shops, and a restaurant. The works have been preceded by archaeological excavations, thus increasing knowledge of the earlier structures, and an educational service has been established. Developments continue under the present abbot, David Charlesworth.

Although in some ways the two communities, of Buckfast and Buckfastleigh may appear different - one the village, the other the town - many Buckfast people regard themselves as very much part of the community of Buckfastleigh. Several of the residents of Buckfast are Roman Catholics, but possibly fewer than was the case earlier in the 1900s. Whilst in the new Abbey's early days there was sometimes a sense of disparagement, or suspicion, between those respectively viewed as 'Papists' and 'Protestants' - though there were many acts of kindness too - today there is much greater understanding, close feeling and co-operation between the denominations. A recent example of this ecumenism was the service of commemoration of the fiftieth anniversary of VE Day, held in the Abbey Church in May 1995, in which Buckfastleigh's other congregations participated - an occasion that was seen as very moving.

See page 94 for notes on Chapter 3.

4
≋ HOLY TRINITY CHURCH ≋

It is certain that there was a church building on the present site of Holy Trinity by the mid thirteenth century (the first vicar, Walvanus, is recorded in 1263-4) and possible that one may have existed even earlier. Evidence of this is suggested by the design of the Norman font, of twelfth century style, although this may have been brought here from elsewhere.[1] The tower dates from the thirteenth century, and the chancel and transepts also possibly originate from this time, with aisles and chancel chapels being further developed in the fifteenth century. An architectural survey of Holy Trinity, prepared in 1991-92, provides a detailed description of its fabric and furnishings prior to the 1992 fire (see Appendix 6). Worship and liturgy would, of course, have been Roman Catholic, under the Church of Rome, until the Reformation of the mid sixteenth century.

The Revd Robert Bradford, vicar in the late 1750s, in his response to Dean Milles, stated that the church was dedicated to St Peter, but this must have been a momentary lapse since it has always been dedicated to, and known to be dedicated to the Trinity.[2] Bradford described the church as being in the form of a cross, 115ft in length, 60ft in breadth, and consisting of a nave and two aisles, with two cross aisles, divided by two rows of pillars - four on the south and two on the north side. The structure was said to be of stone, roofed with slate, and having at the west end a square tower 80ft high surmounted by an octagonal spire. Although there are records of repairs carried out from 1712, a presentment by the rural dean in 1758 suggests that the church was in a poor state of repair - a view that was resented and questioned by the vicar. Nevertheless, a century later White's Directory of 1850

refers to the restoration which the church underwent in 1844 'after long being in a shamefully neglected state'.

The restoration carried out between 1844-1846 was extensive and necessitated closure of the church for two years and two months.[3] To mastermind this work, the parish turned to John Hayward of Exeter, who was a nephew and pupil of Charles Barry, and who is today viewed as the leading Devon church architect in the Victorian period. Then in his late thirties, he went on to promote the Gothic revival style in numerous

An early drawing of Holy Trinity Church is to be found in the manuscript of Dean Milles's questionnaire, dating back to the 1750s. Redrawn from the original.

Holy Trinity Church in 1981. (Dr J.H. Wildman).

church restoration projects in the Exeter diocese. The main contractor for the work at Holy Trinity was the Buckfastleigh firm of Abbot and Willcocks. The cost is believed to have been around £1,300-£1,400, financed by income from the parish lands that had earlier been bequeathed for such purposes.[4]

In this major reconstruction[5] walls were raised 5ft in order to take new roofs of Welsh slate with crested ridge tiles. The wagon roof of the chancel[6] was, how-ever, retained at the lower level, and a nineteenth century foliated cross[7] mounted on the coped gable end above the three-light Early English style east window. (Another cross, mounted on the gable of the south porch, was believed to be of Early English origin.).[8] The upper part of the spire, which had long been truncated (believed due to a lightning strike) was also renewed and raised a further 38ft, giving a total height for tower and spire of 135ft.[9] Walls were smoothly cement rendered, apart from the tower which had earlier been roughcast, and the spire was similarly finished. Granite dressings featured in the work, which included renewal of most of the window mullions.

Internally, previously applied limewash was scraped from the octagonal piers of the arcades, which displayed double hollow chamfered arches and capitals. In the north aisle two new granite piers - monoliths - were added,[10] thus apparently enlarging that side of the church and bringing the number of its pillars to four, equalling the number on the south side as previously counted by Robert Bradford. Plastered ceilings were removed and the open roof exposed. A gallery at the church's west end was removed, and in the body of the church former box pews were apparently reduced in height and provided with doors, and their arrangement altered so that they faced east.[11] A former Grecian altar piece was replaced with a reredos of wood, flanked by painted texts, and a contemporary carved oak pulpit, by Webber of Exeter, installed. During the restoration work five piscinas (drains for water used for washing the communion vessels)[12] were revealed, and a hagioscope (a squint, to enable a view of the high altar from the south aisle) noted between the north transept and the chancel.

The overall effect of Hayward's scheme had been to 're-medievalise' Holy Trinity in keeping with the spirit of the Gothic Revival movement, and the result was greeted with enthusiasm. For example, the Exeter Diocesan Architectural Society (of which Hayward was a leading light) gave a glowing report in 1848:

The appearance of the restored church is such as should give courage to all zealous in the cause of these Holy Houses of Prayer. The general effect is exceedingly good - the height, ample aisle, unincumbered (sic) chancel, very striking. The roofs (lean-to in the aisle, and richer in the chancel) are of oak,

and stained wood, open, and substantial - after Mr Hayward's plan. The pews are equal, lower, decent, and of good proportion; and the gallery gone! The happily combined zeal of the Vicar and Churchwardens, aided by land bequeathed in olden times for the purpose, have effected all this, and most gratifying must it be to the parishioners at large.

But the church was not long to remain in an untroubled state.[13] On Tuesday 8 May 1849 arsonists with iron bars broke into the building through a window in the north aisle and started a fire in the vestry, which, together with the parish chest, was destroyed. Part of the roof of the north aisle was also destroyed and the communion table severely damaged. The fire engine was summoned, and the firemen, together with reported hundreds of parishioners who brought water, worked hard to contain and quench the blaze. By their efforts the damage was limited to an estimated cost of £100.[14] Evidently repairs were soon carried out, and by 1850 a new altar was in position to replace the one destroyed, paid for by gifts of some of the parishioners.

During the second half of the nineteenth century moves were being made towards providing a chapel-of-ease in the town area of Buckfastleigh for the greater convenience of the town's increasing population in attending Sunday evening and other services. (It appears from a diocesan inventory of 1553 that there may then have been a small chapel-of-ease somewhere in the Market Street area - at one stage there may, in fact, have been two - having two small bells. But in the 1750s Bradford reported that there were no chapels-of-ease). In 1858-9 attempts were made to raise money for the venture, but these were not then fully successful, and the matter was delayed until the 1890s. The building of St Luke's Church was completed in 1894.[15]

The chancel and altar of Holy Trinity Church. (Dr J.H. Wildman).

An early view of the church interior.

In 1897 a chancel renovation was carried out at Holy Trinity, paid for by Mr Fleming of Bigadon. Possibly this resulted in the scene as portrayed in an old photograph believed to have been taken around 1900. The plastered walls of the chancel are shown to be decorated with stencil patterns, and also a stencilled frieze and dado. Even more interesting, the pulpit is seen on the north side of the chancel, with an extended stairway and rail. It was probably as the result of a faculty of 1910, granted for removal of the organ in the north transept, re-seating of the chancel with alteration of the floor level, and re-seating of the chapel at the east end of the north aisle, that the pulpit was moved to the south side.

The Organ

A new organ had been installed in 1899, built by George Hawkins of Newton Abbot and paid for by Mr

Joseph Hamlyn. It is said to have been sited in the north transept, with choir stalls close by, but the exact position is uncertain. Great rejoicings accompanied the occasion of its inauguration on 20 May 1899. A tent was erected in a field adjoining the churchyard in which local dignitaries and others attended a luncheon, but unfortunately rain marred the day. This organ was later taken down the hill and installed in St Luke's Church to replace a small portable one, when, in 1911, a newer organ, given by Mr Robert Fleming, and choir stalls donated by Mrs Fleming in memory of John Fleming, were provided for Holy Trinity.[16] These were dedicated on the afternoon of Wednesday 20 September 1911 by the Bishop of Exeter.[17] The organ was built by Hele and Company of Plymouth, and the choir stalls carved by Herbert Read of Exeter from designs by Sir Charles Nicholson. Following the dedication service the organ was opened by Mr A. E. Wilshire FRCO, organist of Wimborne Minster, who then gave a recital.

The Bells

As has already been said, after the Dissolution of the Monasteries, the five bells of Buckfast Abbey were apparently bought from the abbey's new owner, Sir Thomas Dennys, by Buckfastleigh parishioners, for £33.15s. The idea of their having all been in use at the abbey as church bells, and that they were immediately hung in the parish church tower as they were received, has been questioned by the noted authority on bells and ringing, the Revd John Scott.[18] Mr Scott points out that the Cistercians were not supposed to indulge themselves with elaborate trimmings, and that, although there was some relaxation in the fifteenth century, they would have been allowed only

The Holy Trinity church bells awaiting rehanging before their dedication in 1935.

two bells - five would have been quite out of order. He suggests that possibly the bells were quite small ones, and that one or two may have been added to the three or four which the church would undoubtedly have already possessed, with two hung in a then existing chapel-of-ease in the town and the other in the 'common house' (later removed to the vicarage). (The 1553 diocesan inventory mentions that there were five bells in the church, one in the common house and two in the chapel). There are other suggested possibilities about the disposition of the abbey bells, which probably featured in subsequent re-castings.

Buckfastleigh churchwardens' accounts from 1712 to 1794, on which Mr Scott has provided explanations and comments, show that there was re-casting of the fourth bell by John Stadler in 1712, and he explains that its description as the fourth and not the great bell shows that by this time there were already five. There was a further re-casting - apparently of the full set - by Ambrose Gooding of Plymouth in 1743, and another in 1793, possibly after an interval of only fifty years, on account of cracks that may have resulted from Gooding's casting. Apparently in 1794 a treble bell was added by re-casting the one previously at the vicarage, making a ring of six. The 1793 casting was carried out by Thomas Bilbie, and the bells may have been broken up and taken to his foundry at Cullompton for the work to be done. At other times it was customary for casting of church bells to take place in the churchyard or in an adjacent field, where a shed, furnace, and casting-pit would be set up. The molten metal - roughly three parts copper to one part tin - would be poured into moulds, made from clay, horse dung and sand, with hair and sometimes hay added to bind the mixture. It is believed that at Buckfastleigh a convenient supply of clay could be obtained from a nearby field. It was important to keep the moulds dry and protected from weather as, if damp, they would explode when the hot metal was poured into them. Sometimes a bell would prove defective and would have to be broken up and re-cast, and then, in order to protect against theft or embezzlement by the bellfounder of the valuable metal, security had to be provided. Watch also needed to be kept overnight when cast bells were cooling down and the Buckfastleigh accounts show that, among men employed, Will Burstow and John Burstow (probably the churchwarden) carried out this function.

The fourth bell of the six was re-cast in 1844 by Hambling of Blackawton, this being the time of Hayward's restoration of the church[19] (see Appendix 4).

In September 1910, during the incumbency of the Revd Frank Nesbitt, the bells were rehung in a new iron frame by Harley Stoke and Son of Woodleigh (see Appendix 3). They were dedicated on 17 December and thanksgiving for the work was made during evensong, for which a printed order of service was provided.[20] It is interesting to note some of the phrases within the series of prayers, quaint by today's style, but nevertheless conveying fine sentiments, and spiritual truths which could still be faithfully prayed for today. They include:

... grant that through this generation, and through those that are to come, the bells of this Thine House may continually call together Thy faithful people to prayer and worship... Grant... that whosoever shall be called by the sound of these bells... and finally may have a portion in the new song, and among the harpers harping with their harps ...whosoever, by reason of sickness, or any other necessity, shall be shut up, so that he cannot come unto the House of the Lord, may in heart and mind thither ascend... that they, who with their outward ears shall hear the sound of these bells, may be aroused inwardly in their spirits, and draw nigh unto Thee ...'.

Several years later the condition of the spire was causing anxiety. At a meeting of the Parochial Church Council (PCC) on 1 November 1932[21] Mr R. Jackson reported that the spire was badly warped from about half way down, and that the whole of the plastering in the top 9ft was cracking badly. It was suggested that the top should be taken down and rebuilt and that the iron finial (surmounting decoration) should be securely screwed down to cross bars built into the spire's stonework. The price of the work (except for materials), comprising: erection of scaffolding, taking down the summit iron cross and the top 9ft of stonework, rebuilding with either new or old stone and replastering, cleaning and applying three coats of paint to the fillet, and re-fixing the finial and the lightning conductor, was estimated at £86. However, by March 1933 V. G. Morris Ltd, the firm undertaking the work, had revised their estimate due to more of the spire being removed, and noting the new figure as approximately £200.[22] How this was to be raised was a matter of concern. The Feoffees (trustees of certain local charitable funds) had agreed to finance the original estimate, and various means of raising the remainder were considered. This was achieved through the holding of a bazaar, whist drives and a jumble sale, by the sale of 'brick cards', and a subscription list. The work was completed later in the year, the chosen method being to build up the top of the spire with 9in brickwork, with one or two solid stones at the top, afterwards plastered over to match existing work. The iron summit cross was broken up by Messrs Willcocks and Sons and re-cast in their foundry in May,[23] and in July the PCC agreed to accept Willcocks' estimate of £13.14s.6d for re-gilding the cross with gold leaf.[24]

At the July meeting of the PCC it was suggested that the bells, which had not been rung during the works to the spire, should receive attention and expert advice be obtained regarding certain defects.[25] In December the captain of the ringers, Mr Stancombe, reported that the tenor bell was badly cracked, and Mr Narramore gave a detailed report on damage found and considered that all the bells should be carefully examined. On 8 March 1934[26] reports and estimates were received from bellfounders Gillett and Johnson of Croydon, and John Taylor and Sons of Loughborough, and a sub-committee was formed to study these in detail. The matter was further considered and discussed by the PCC on 10 July, when it was agreed to give the work to Taylors. The vicar, The Revd H. Mylchreest, then gave the council some 'startling news' which was to allay the anxiety of how the 'ways and means' could be found. The scheme was to be the generous gift of 'a lady and gentleman who were very interested in their church'. It did not take council members many minutes to jump to the fact that the couple were Mr and Mrs R. E. Churchward of Hillside, who had been benefactors of both Holy Trinity and St Luke's for many years. Taylors' estimate for re-casting and re-hanging the six bells with entirely new fittings in a new strong massive cast-iron framework on a double set of foundation girders was £376, a new framework made for eight bells £28, eight new main wheels £20, and two new treble bells £122, making a total of £546. The church was now, therefore, to have a full peal of eight bells. The gift was also to include the rebuilding of the damaged portion of the inside of the tower, and Messrs Jackson and Son were asked to give an estimate for this work and for carpentry and masonry in connection with the bells (totalled later as £61.4s.0d). Great enthusiasm was shown at the meeting for the 'magnificent gift', a hearty vote of thanks was passed, and the decision taken to apply immediately for the necessary faculty.

During the autumn the work proceeded and at the November meeting of the PCC[27] the vicar enthusiastically announced that the bells had arrived from

The Rev. H. Mylchreest with the Holy Trinity churchwardens and ringers at the time of the dedication of the bells in 1935. The author's grandfather, John Warren, is second from the left, seated.

Taylors' foundry. He expressed delight at their appearance and considered that the work had been well done. Arrangements were made for the opening event, which was to take place on Saturday 12 January 1935. There was to be a tea following the service and a committee was appointed to arrange this, chaired by my grandmother, Mrs Warren, and including also Mrs Churchward, Mrs Mylchreest and other notable ladies in the parish. Mrs Churchward was a close friend of both my grandmothers and she was also my mother's godmother. We were invited to attend the service and to meet the Lord Bishop of Exeter afterwards at tea in the Town Hall. I was sent my own individual invitation! While the work on the tower and ringing chamber had been going on, the wall at the centre of the west end of the church had been screened off by a huge tarpaulin. I remember my father telling me, while it was still there, that the next time I came to church I should be able to *see* the ringers. And now, so I could. Instead of ringing from floor level, as previously, the ringers were now accommodated at higher level in an open-sided ringing chamber above a choir vestry with oak screening. I was entranced. Moreover, it was also now possible to hear the captain's instructions as the changes were called out, but not very clearly down in the body of the church, and I used to imagine phrases that were quite different from the words actually used.

The occasion, which certainly marked a high peak in the history of the church on the hill, was reported in two and a half columns of the broadsheet *Western Guardian* of 17 January. It was undoubtedly a fine service with organ and choir, attended by nine visiting clergy and with a full congregation that included over 100 ringers from other parishes. After he had dedicated the bells, the Bishop (the Rt Revd Lord William Cecil) gave a lengthy address in rambling style and containing some terminology of views that would not be countenanced today. At the conclusion of the service the bells were rung by the Buckfastleigh ringers: Messrs J. Stancombe (captain), T.H. Baker, J.W. Wood, E.L. Carne, J. H. Cole, W.H. Narramore, F.J. Emmett and S.E. Stockman. Ringing continued through the evening until 9pm with other ringers taking turns. (For details of the bells including the inscriptions on them see Appendix 4.).

The next day, Sunday, following the morning service a tablet given by the parishioners and recording the gift, and fixed to the wall of the choir vestry, was unveiled by Mr Churchward, accompanied by Mrs Churchward. Sadly, however, the bells' benefactress was not to hear them for long. Less than three months after the dedication, on 8 April, Mrs Mary Churchward died suddenly, and the parish mourned the loss of a good friend.

The Font[28]

The impressive Norman font (at which I was baptised on 6 March 1927) is believed to date from the twelfth century, being of the earliest honeysuckle type. The large cup-shaped bowl of red sandstone carries a scroll

The Norman font prior to its removal to the South Transept.

pattern, with coiled rope-like carving around the top, below a plain lip. The bowl, set on a cylindrical stem, was surrounded by four added shafts of marble with varied Norman type capitals, which may have been removed from the sedilia (priests' seats in the chancel). Surmounted by a domed cover (believed to have been late eighteenth century) the font in earlier days stood in the south-west area of the church, somewhat awkwardly close against a pillar. Some parishioners (including my grandmother) for long held the view that this placing was not worthy of the Sacrament of Baptism, and that it should be moved to a more suitable position. Accordingly, after a faculty had been obtained, a new baptistry area was established, still on the south side, but farther east, and the font removed there. The new arrangement was dedicated by the Revd H. Mylchreest on a return visit in November 1954. The work was carried out by the building firm of PCC member Mr Philip Jackson, whose family also gave oak seats for the baptistry in memory of his father, Robert Jackson. (Small copper plates commemorating members of the family and the gift were later rescued from the remains of the 1992 fire and are in the treasured possession of the Jacksons' descendant, Mrs Julie Soul).

Stained Glass

The coloured glass of the windows as it survived until the fire of 1992 reflected the nineteenth century enthusiasm for restoration, with no medieval glazing remaining intact. Much of the glass was designed by the Beer family in Exeter (later to trade under the name of Beer and Driffield). Robert Beer was the earliest Victorian artist to be working in stained glass in Devon and the presence of Beer glass at Holy Trinity (as with the choice of John Hayward as architect for the 1840s restoration scheme) shows that the parish was using the services of the best local craftsmen in the county.

Most of the windows depicted biblical scenes and had been given in memory of various clergy and parishioners. They suffered from bomb blast during the Second World War and the backgrounds of several of the windows were removed, leaving isolated figures with some saints' heads lost. The war damage authority paid for replacement with plain glass. (For details of the stained glass see Appendix 3).

Memorials

When the Revd Robert Bradford was asked by Dean Milles in the 1750s what memorials or inscriptions the church contained that were earlier than 1600 he replied firmly 'none'. Regarding coats of arms he noted that there were many 'against the pulpit, too many to be mentioned here'. However, these apparently disappeared when the new pulpit was installed in 1846. Numerous memorials and gifts were placed in the church, however, after 1600, besides those already described (see Appendix 3). There were inscribed floor slabs and wall tablets as well as further fabric, goods and ornaments, including the brass eagle lectern, which dated from the early 1900s and was given by the Tanner family of Hawson Court, and the later wooden reredos dedicated in 1920. One of the most interesting memorials was an ancient altar stone, with three crosses inscribed on it, which was later used as a tombstone in the nave, inscribed 1653 and 1693. In the twentieth century this was raised and set on its end against the inside south wall of the church. (Sadly, smashed by intruding vandals since the 1992 fire). Also notable was the interior war memorial, of wood, just inside the south door on the east side (see Appendix 5). In the porch another board, placed here in 1931, the gift of Miss Mabel Hamlyn, listed the parish's incumbents (Appendix 1), and also here were parish stocks of earlier times - a source of fascination to many children and others.

As already mentioned (page 22) from 1894 to 1920 a church school existed at Buckfast. After its closure the building was bought by Mr R. Fleming and conveyed by him and wife, via the Diocesan Board of Finance, to Buckfastleigh Church in 1931, for use as a mission room. An altar and vessels were dedicated but a screen could be put across to enable the building to be used for purposes other than services. There was much enthusiasm over the gift and much help given in repairing and redecorating by the people of Buckfast, who also subscribed to a memorial tablet placed in the building, which was named the Violet Evelyn Church Institute, in memory of the Flemings' daughter.[29] Mrs Fleming unveiled the tablet and expressed her gratitude in 1932. The Violet Evelyn Institute fulfilled its purpose for almost sixty years, latterly with services held regularly on Sunday afternoons. Its use dwindled however, and in 1990 the building was acquired by the Abbey and now forms a centre for people on retreat and other visitors to the Abbey. When this happened the altar, vessels and ornaments were taken up to the church on the hill, and used there as a basis for a 'Violet Evelyn chapel' in the north aisle.

The Churchyard

The huge churchyard, with its lovely views to north and west, has a great many tombstones, which may provide interest to those seeking family or local history (see Appendix 6 for a description of those that have been listed). Also, just inside the south entrance gate is the granite war memorial, a fine cross with inscriptions that include the names of those of the parish who died in the Services in the First and Second World Wars. (See Appendix 5). This memorial was dedicated on a fine Sunday afternoon, 12 July 1920.[30] A large crowd attended, and around 100 local men who had served in the 1914-18 war (including my father, John Robert Hoare Warren, who had been a 2nd Lieut. in

The War Memorial in Holy Trinity churchyard. It was erected in 1920 to commemorate those who fell in the Great War of 1914-18.

the King's Own Royal Lancaster Regiment) paraded, marching to the church from Barter's Bridge in the town, headed by the Town Band. Besides the vicar, the Revd John Lucas, the Wesleyan and Congregational ministers also participated in the service, the church choir attended, a short address was given by Col. F. K. Windeatt of Totnes, and the memorial was unveiled by Miss Mabel Hamlyn of Fullaford.

A feature of greater antiquity, in the eastern area of the churchyard, is the ruin of a medieval chapel. Virtually nothing is known of its history, but it is considered to have been a chantry chapel. It has been conjectured that the chapel may have been built by the Cistercian monks in the early days of the abbey, or else erected for private use, but these are only speculations. Probably the remains date from the thirteenth century, but the possibility of their being the remnants of an original church on the site is discounted by the fact that tower and chancel structures of the actual church are of contemporary, if not earlier date. By the mid eighteenth century, according to the Revd Robert Bradford's reply to Dean Milles, the building was already a ruin, and it has apparently changed little in the two centuries or so since then.

In 1990 a fabric survey of the chapel, funded by English Heritage, was carried out by the Exeter

The ruined chapel which stands in the churchyard to the east of the church. The ruin has been repaired since this photograph was taken.

Museum's Archaeological Field Unit, and the report, by S. R. Blaylock, describes the structure in full detail.[31] The building stone is substantially grey limestone from nearby local sources, but various other types, identifiable with more distant Devon sources, are included, with the exception - in primary use - of granite. On the internal walls, where plaster covering the rubble work has survived, traces of red and yellowish paint have been found as vertical and horizontal lines giving the effect of 'false ashlar' painting, a common type of cosmetic decoration which has also been noted covering high quality masonry in the south tower of Exeter Cathedral.

Much curiosity has been aroused over the years by the large roofed tomb structure situated just a few feet from the church's south porch. Known locally as 'the sepulchre', the penthouse covers the raised tomb of members of the Cabell family, lords of the manor of Buckfastleigh in the seventeenth century. (See Chapter 2.).[32] It was built by the third Richard of the family

The Cabell tomb which stands just outside the south porch of the church.

around 1656, but contains the remains of the first Richard Cabell to live in Buckfastleigh (died 1612 or 1613) and of his wife Susannah who died in 1597, and of their son, the second Richard following his death in 1655. The third Richard died in 1672, at the age of fifty. There is no certainty as to whether or not he was also buried in the tomb, but his apparent life-style gave rise to legendary stories about him. Besides building the tomb, the third Richard also built the manor house at Brook where he lived in style. Among appointments that he held was that of Sheriff of Devon in 1664. Possibly he was a hard man, and he acquired a reputation of alleged immorality. There may have been other people for whom building up a fierce reputation for Richard Cabell could have been advantageous. My Coulton grandmother who, through her long life had listened to tales told by older people of Buckfastleigh, attributed some of them to the practice of body snatching (to sell for medical research) which was apparently rife in the early nineteenth century in Buckfastleigh churchyard with the quick getaway facility via Fairies' Hall to the main road. It was thought that accounts of a laughing 'Old Cabell' passing that way in a coach led by headless horses, or with a headless coachman, and other stories, may have been invented to deter inconvenient witnesses of the illicit grave robbings, or, perhaps, to discourage local people from lifting turnips from farmers' fields near Church Cross. The square sepulchre, roofed with slate, was provided with bars - it was said 'to keep Cabell in'. Even in the present century I remember being told how, if I walked around the sepulchre seven times, and put my fingers through the bars, the devil (or Cabell) would bite them. Sadly, in recent years, the sepulchre has been disgracefully vandalised, but has undergone some restoration, including the fitting of a new substantial door by the Dartmoor National Park Authority (DNPA).

The procession at the dedication of the churchyard extension in 1935. The Bishop of Exeter is largely obscured by his chaplain, who follows the two churchwardens.

By 1933 the churchyard was almost full of graves, and at its meeting of 20 January the PCC considered enlarging the burial ground.[33] Discussion followed, but possibly because of the ensuing preoccupation with the spire and bells, the matter was delayed until 1934, when the decision was made to proceed.[34] Negotiations followed with the Coulton family, owners of the adjacent field, for purchase of an acre of the land, in what was considered a 'good offer'. Later it was announced that the cost of the churchyard extension was to be the gift of the Misses Mabel and Violet Hamlyn, in memory of their parents, Joseph and Elizabeth Green Hamlyn. Arrangements proceeded and on Saturday afternoon, 26 October 1935, for the second time in the year Bishop Cecil of Exeter came to Buckfastleigh and performed the consecration. The well-attended service was described by the vicar, Mr Mylchreest, as a memorable one, and he was 'very grateful at the way parishioners showed their appreciation of what had been done'. My Warren grandmother noted in her diary '... a full church and big crowd in the yard. Bishop preached very well'. In the 1980s, during the incumbency of the Revd Richard Steele-Perkins, the burial ground was further extended.

Other features surrounding the churchyard are its western lych gate and near the gates stone stiles set in the surrounding walls. They were for use when sheep were enclosed to graze the grass, and the gates were locked. Apparently once, when a bride arrived for her marriage, the gates were thus locked, and she had to climb over the stile in her wedding dress.

Outside the west gate, across the road, were stable buildings, and beside them, upping stocks for the convenience of riders mounting or dismounting from their horses. As a child I remember Mr John Rowland, co-churchwarden with my grandfather, arriving in his horse and trap, or pony and jingle, which he would leave here in the stable while he attended the Sunday service (see Appendix 6).

See page 95 for notes on Chapter 4.

Mid-Devon Advertiser

Incorporating Mid-Devon Times   Established 1863   Price 24p

Newton Abbot 53555. Advertising 55566.   **FRIDAY, July 24, 1992**

Future of church in doubt

Cast-iron radiators were all that remained unharmed in the burned-out shell of Holy Trinity Church, as firemen continue to damp down on Tuesday morning.

The remaining shell of the church as seen by photographer Chris Bryan from the top of the tower 11 hours after the fire was believed to have started. Heat was still emanating from the stonework as he climbed the tower.

Blaze guts 13th century Holy Trinity

THE future of Holy Trinity Parish Church, Buckfastleigh, is in doubt after it was gutted by fire on Tuesday.

The Bishop of Plymouth, the Rt Rev Richard Hawkins, said it was not urgent for the church authorities to make a decision on its future.

The daughter church St Luke's would cope with services and other church activities until experts from the insurers and others called in by church authorities assessed the full extent of the damage and could give advice.

'We're very fortunate to have the daughter church. This means there is no ur-

By
ALAN HEATHER
and
JOHN BALMENT

gent pressure to make a long-term decision,' he said.

The Bishop said that while it was up to the townsfolk of Buckfastleigh to do what they thought best, it was too early to consider setting up an appeal fund. This should wait until it was possible to make decisions on the church's future.

Commenting on rumours that some kind of Black Magic ritual in the church had caused the fire, which started near the altar, the Bishop said:

'At present there is no evidence at all of that having been the case, but we can't discount it altogether.

There have been many other incidents like this where Black Magic has been blamed and it has not been.'

A spokeswoman for the Church Commissioners said the decision whether or not to rebuild a church depended on individual circumstances. The need for a place to worship was the paramount consideration, over and above financial ones.

'If there is a local need

● Turn to Back Page

One of many newspaper reports of the 1992 fire.

54

5
⚜ THE FIRE OF 1992 ⚜

In the early evening of Tuesday 21 July 1992, at the start of the BBC South-West news, I heard the headline 'one of Devon's prettiest churches is destroyed by fire'. Until the report followed I wondered which, given the description, this could be. And then, suddenly, pictures of a church very familiar to me - but in ruins, black, and smouldering, were on the screen. This was Holy Trinity Church, Buckfastleigh - the church for generations of my family, and of my baptism.[1] The advance headline had never given me any clue of the identity - the description just did not fit. Beautiful in its line, but plainly rendered, the church could have been truthfully described as 'prominent', 'highly-situated', even 'noble', or indeed, 'cherished', but 'pretty' is not a term either I or many would have used. My first thought was for my ninety-seven year-old aunt, Edith, whose life had been deeply involved with the church and who had helped care for it lovingly over very many years, and I telephoned her. She, like most of the people of Buckfastleigh, was stunned and devastated, and somewhat bemused that everyone seemed to have been telephoning her. 'I don't know what they think I can do about it' she said desolately. And the following week, when I went over to Buckfastleigh and saw the smoke-stained, ravaged, desecrated structure, silently and forlornly standing under a brilliant blue sky, with the indignity of being tied around with yellow tapes and boarded up to prevent access, it all seemed so incredibly sad.

Ours was, of course, but one family of many who felt so sharply the sadness of the event. The talk in Buckfastleigh had been of little else. According to subsequent investigations, around midnight the padlock of the main door had been broken open, evidently with the aid of a crowbar, and also the vestry window had been smashed prior to the blaze. It was believed that the fire began shortly after midnight. Apparently it was started under the altar and then smouldered its way towards the wooden structure of the organ, where it erupted into an inferno. The hilltop glow was noticed by Ashburton Police Constable John Fisher on routine patrol at 4.11 a.m., and the alarm was quickly raised. Just after 4 o'clock a sound of banging (probably cracking slates) had woken a nearby resident, Mr Martin Hayward, who was horrified to look out and see a silhouette of the steeple outlined against the flames. By the time he reached the church, half the roof had gone. The vicar, the Revd Paul Wilson, was roused from his bed within minutes of the alarm and was quickly on the scene, where in addition to the fire brigades, many people gathered.

When the first fire crew, from Buckfastleigh, arrived and realised the immensity of the blaze, they immediately radioed for back-up support, which brought aid from Ashburton, Bovey Tracey, Totnes, Ivybridge, Newton Abbot, and Torquay, until eventually seventy fire-fighters were involved. A major problem was a lack of adequate water on the site, the nearest hydrant being on the main road a quarter of a mile away. It was necessary to set up a relay system consisting of a chain of thirty-eight 70ft hoses from three different points in the valley below, with intermediate pumping to boost pressure and force the water uphill. For local firemen, with memories of being married in the church, or of other family associations with it, the operation was emotionally shattering.

For some hours firemen fought the blaze, and the morning was well advanced before the smouldering

A close-up view showing the extent of the fire damage taken two days after the fire as part of a detailed photographic record of Holy Trinity Church. (Royal Commission on the Historical Monuments of England. © Crown Copyright).

Top left: Holy Trinity Church as it was before the fire of 20/21 July 1992. (Dartmoor National Park Authority). *Lower left: A photographer records one of the historic memorials on the walls of the fire-shattered church two days after the fire.* (Devon County Council). *Right: A view of the church interior looking east towards the chancel. The chancel arch visible in this photo was subsequently demolished on safety grounds.* (Devon County Council).

remains could be investigated. The shell of the building was still standing, also the porch, and the vestry - with its safe containing documents and precious vessels intact. The tower and spire, although blackened, still rose above the scene. Thanks to the strong iron framework installed in the tower in 1934 the eight bells were still in position. Had the frame been of wood, and burnt, the bells would have crashed to the ground and smashed. The firemen took great pains to keep water away from the bells, to avoid cracking them. Concern and sympathy came from near and far. The abbot and community of Buckfast Abbey offered sympathy and prayers for the parishioners of Buckfastleigh. In his message Abbot David Charlesworth wrote: 'The parish church of Holy Trinity was a very visible sign of our common Christian heritage and the monastic community shares this loss. The Church of Christ is not made of bricks and mortar but of living stones that are the men, women and children of the parish. We wish to show support by emphasising wholeheartedly our common Christian faith. Perhaps this tragedy will provide us all with an opportunity to strengthen the bonds that already unite the local community'.

During the day, while many Buckfastleigh people came sadly to view the scorched remains, others with authority entered within to take account of the extent of the incineration - a dangerous procedure since parts of the surviving structure had become unsafe. One who came, with his wife and one or two other helpers, was long-term church member and former churchwarden Mr John Gill. They rescued several surviving items, including the stocks from the porch, and the bishop's chair and safe with its contents from the vicar's vestry (they were not suitably equipped on this visit to take away the vestry table and near-empty chest, both of which were shortly stolen by intruders). The floor of the church was littered with fallen mason-

ry and charred beams, though the old iron radiators still stood their ground in gaunt isolation. Due to the intense heat the pillars within the building had suffered badly. Their stonework in places had been reduced to flakes and was disintegrating, and splitting had occurred, caused by expansion of the mica constituent of the granite. A necessary safety measure, carried out the next day, was demolition of the tall chancel arch.

The decorated Norman font had been literally blown to bits by the ferocity of the fire and was at first thought to be beyond repair. But its scattered fragments were carefully collected together by Deborah Griffiths, the DNPA archaeologist, who played a key role in salvaging as many of the historic fittings of the church as possible. County Archaeologist, Simon Timms, youngest son of the former vicar, was among the rescuers of items from the vestry, taking parish records for emergency conservation in the Devon Record Office.

The finding of a brass cross, scorched and buckled, by Buckfastleigh's non-stipendary curate the Revd John Irwin, seemed however a symbol of hope, as also were two fragments of stained glass, each depicting a white dove, which, amazingly, had survived and were rescued from the ashes.

In succeeding days the site was visited and surveyed by representatives of various bodies: insurance assessors; Teignbridge District Council; English Heritage's structural engineer Keith Western - who had to prepare a report for decisions on possible grants towards restoration of the Grade I listed building; officers from the Royal Commission on Historic Monuments; the Diocesan authorities; Devon County Council; the DNPA; and others. The police continued their intense investigations for some months, but no clues or information were sufficient to lead to identification of the arsonists. Although the media sensationalized possible links with 'black magic' and fictional connections, the police maintain that they never found any evidence of satanical activities among the ruins - the act was seen as sheer vandalism. While the likelihood of a solution of the crime has faded, the relevant police file is nevertheless still open.

In early August, by which time scaffolding had been erected to support sections of the church walls and pillars (paid for by English Heritage), the bells were carefully removed from the tower by a specialist bell hanger, Arthur Fidler. They were taken to Buckfast Abbey for safe keeping until the time when they could be replaced. The conservation and re-erection of the font was organised and paid for (£2,950) by the DNPA, with Alison Hopper at Exeter Museum carrying out the initial conservation work. The many shattered pieces were reassembled by the specialist firm, Nimbus. With assistance from the DNPA the restored font, weighing 3cwt, was placed in St Luke's Church in August 1993, where it has since been used for baptisms.

Meanwhile, following the fire, a firm of historic building consultants, Keystone, contracted by English Heritage and the DNPA, produced an initial archaeological evaluation of the damaged building. Keystone was then contracted by English Heritage to make a more detailed study of the remains, apart from the chancel and tower. A firm of building contractors was engaged to clear debris and strip plaster, two specialist archaeologists were sub-contracted from Exeter Museum Archaeological Field Unit to record masonry, and an independent archaeologist, Stewart Brown, employed as consultant. Rebecca Child of English Heritage, DNPA archaeologist Deborah Griffiths, and Buckfastleigh-born architect Ronald Weekes met on the site, and it was decided to store carefully all stone rubble and dressed stone for examination and possible later re-use. The remaining structure was recorded by drawings and photographs, although it was realised that there was still considerable archaeological potential for investigation. The way forward was discussed by a parish working party which met at intervals up to December 1993 and, starting in 1995, work to the tower and spire proceeded in the hands of local builders Blight and Scoble. New flooring was installed in the various levels of the tower and a reinforced glazed screen provided against a slightly higher ringing gallery to enable ringers to be again visible from below. In the autumn of 1995 the bells were taken back to Loughborough for annealing and retuning at the works for John Taylor and Sons, and were eventually returned to Buckfastleigh and rehung in the tower. Their first official ringing was for the passing of 1995 and the coming-in of 1996 - a sound that brought joy to many.

In subsequent months, clearing of the church's internal area continued and by the spring of 1996 a restored sense of peace could be experienced within the walls. The outer wall structures are mainly intact, although reduced in height by the removal of the 5ft of masonry added in the 1840s. Internally, of the eight pillars in the nave arcades which suffered badly, the two Victorian monoliths were worst affected and too cracked to be retained. The other six pillars have, however, been secured with steel pins and thus saved. On 2 June - Trinity Sunday - the first service for parishioners since the tragedy was held in a roofless church.

Thus far, repair work has proceeded under the direction of Ronald Weekes in accordance with his aim of retaining as much as possible of the church's ancient structure. The Revd Paul Wilson left the parish in January 1996, following which Buckfastleigh was without a vicar for several months. A new incumbent, the Revd John Rowland was instituted on 4 October 1996 and, at the time of writing, further plans must await his views and those of others on whom decisions rest.

See page 95 for notes on Chapter 5.

Front page of the Parish Magazine as it was when the Rev. H. F. Nesbitt was vicar.

Vol. II.   No. 2.

THE
BUCKFASTLEIGH
PARISH MAGAZINE.

FEBRUARY, 1893.

VICAR :—REV. W. H. B. TUCKER, M.A.
CHURCHWARDENS :—MR. JOHN SYMONS, MR. JOS. HAMLYN
LAY READER:—MR. E. T. WOTTON, Bell House.
ORGANIST:—MR. FRED TOLCHARD.
SEXTON :—MR. JAMES CHAFFE, Wych Cross
SUNDAY SCHOOL { BOYS:—MR. PHILIP JACKSON.
SUPERINTENDENTS { GIRLS:—MISS PATTESON.
SCHOOL LIBRARIAN :—MRS. R. E. CHURCHWARD.

PRICE ONE PENNY.

6
⚘ HOLY TRINITY CHURCH IN THE LIFE OF THE PARISH ⚘

Although doubtless there have been exceptions, many of Buckfastleigh's vicars through the centuries have been dominant figures in the parish and closely associated with its activities. As we have seen, the Revd Robert Bradford in the mid eighteenth century was knowledgeable about the neighbourhood, its people and industries. The (second) Matthew Lowndes in the 1840s was greatly concerned for the well-being and schooling of the children. Another who pressed to 'get things done' in the 1890s and early 1900s, and whose incumbency saw the establishment in 1894 of St Luke's Church, was the Revd W.H.B. Tucker. Then the Revd Frank Nesbitt was a strong and sustaining influence through to the end of the First World War. In turn he appreciated the parishioners' support, as he expressed in a farewell letter in the Parish Magazine when he left for Winkleigh in 1918. His successor was the Revd John Lucas, by whom I was baptised. I do not remember him as vicar, for he moved to East Allington in 1929, but he and his wife and family had a long and continuing friendship with my own family, as was also the case with succeeding clergy. I recall particularly clearly the Revd H. Mylchreest and Mrs Mylchreest, and their family of Joan, Bartie, David and Patience, and also the Revd John Timms, vicar here for thirty-eight years, and Mrs Timms, with their large family. These clergy and their families were respected and warmly regarded in the parish as friends, and were not in the least distanced by always being addressed as 'Mr Mylchreest' or 'Mr Timms', never, to my knowledge, as 'Vicar', 'Father', or by the now more general use of christian names.

The style of worship in the nineteenth century and early part of the twentieth century appears to have

The Rev. H.F. Nesbitt with his pet dog.

61

adhered to the traditional, reformed, Anglican pattern - neither strongly protestant, nor leaning toward Tractarianism. Buckfastleigh had its nonconformist chapels, and the catholic influence was finding its expression in the restored abbey, so Holy Trinity kept to the 'middle of the road'. Later there were gentle swings. Mr Lucas brought in a slightly higher churchmanship, Mr Mylchreest was lower but with a deep spirituality, Mr Timms again raised the level to some degree, introducing a Christmas midnight Communion in 1943, and a monthly choral communion in the 1950s (both bringing the congregation towards the Church's moving trend of the times), and he fostered ecumenical links in the parish and deanery. In more recent incumbencies - those of the Revd Richard Steele-Perksins, and the Revd Paul Wilson, the

Parochial Church Council has described its character of worship as 'open evangelical', to which one might perhaps add: 'with a touch of the charismatic'. The latter years have also brought the benefit of two non-stipendiary priests: the late Revd Eric Jones, who introduced regular healing services, and currently the Revd John Irwin whose ministrations are also greatly valued (for list of vicars see Appendix 1).

The arrangement of Sunday services between Holy Trinity and St Luke's fell into a regular general pattern. The 8 a.m. service of Holy Communion was held at St Luke's, except on Trinity Sunday when it would be 'on the hill'. Matins at 11 a.m., on certain Sundays also with Holy Communion, was at Holy Trinity.

Sometimes there was a children's service on Sunday afternoon at St Luke's, and evensong would take place there in winter, but it would be at Holy Trinity during the summer. At one time this was from the first Sunday in May, but later from the first Sunday in June - or Trinity Sunday if earlier - to the last in September. Generally at Christmas and Easter there would also be a 7 a.m. communion at St Luke's, which was also used for certain mid-week services. Baptisms, marriages, and most funerals would be on the hill. Although in earlier days Sunday evening services would be largely attended, by the 1950s - as elsewhere - fewer people were going to evensong. When the matter was raised at the 1956 Annual Church Meeting the vicar, the Revd John Timms, commented that in America evening services ceased in 1880, and he drew attention to the increasing number of communicants - on the recent Easter Day these had numbered 338, compared with 151 in 1926, 194 in 1930, and 224 in 1939. Also noted were more men than women in the congregation. The number of names on the church electoral roll at that time had risen to 846. (In 1995 it was 123). As already said, Sunday afternoon services were held, too, at Buckfast during the time of the Violet Evelyn Institute.

In 1939 the matter of the uniting of benefices had been discussed locally, possibly to involve the parishes of Rattery and Dean Prior.[1] That August a meeting was held in the Town Hall, which was followed by the general feeling that Buckfastleigh did not want to be united with Dean. The matter was not then proceeded with, but some years later, after the war, it was again under consideration by the Church Commissioners. As a result, in January 1960 a notice of certification of a scheme for uniting the benefices of Buckfastleigh and Dean Prior was placed before the Queen in Council.[2] Thus, from that time, the Vicar of Buckfastleigh has also had responsibility for St George's church and the parish of Dean Prior, and in later years this has necessitated some variations in services times to accommodate both congregations by available clergy.

Buckfastleigh people will have their own visual memories of services in Holy Trinity church. Amongst mine are the light and freshness within the building, shining brasses and the flowers on Easter Sunday, the particular mellow smell and rich sight of corn, vegetables, fruit and flowers at harvest festivals, and of chrysanthemums in late autumn. My eyes (perhaps even as a baby) would be attracted to the red, blue and clear glass of the roundels high in the chancel gable, and when I could read I would study the names on the nearby war memorial board, and look at the pew door on the north side of the nave which proclaimed 'Reserved for the Ringers' - but which they rarely seemed to use. There was a feeling of reverence, and little if any idle chatter before services, but warmth, joy and unity in following the order of service and joining in the singing.

The organist in my early days was Mr Eldred Penny, who completed forty-eight years in that role, from 1924 to 1972. He was succeeded by Mr Budden, and later by Mr Jack Lee, who was also a lay reader. Another organist, and Sunday School teacher, who

Mr Jack Lee at the organ at Advent 1978. The fire of 1992 completely destroyed the organ. (Dr J.H. Wildman).

also became a lay reader and went on to ordination, was Mr Eric Hayman. My aunt, Edith Walters (nee Warren) was often called on as 'reserve organist', even when in her nineties. Until recent times the church choir - like others elsewhere - was composed entirely of men and boys, impressive in numbers and singing as they processed up the aisle from the west choir vestry. Always numerous, and long-serving amongst the choir were members of a family of talented singers - the Bonathans. The late Wilf Joint wrote for me some notes about the choir, of which he was a boy member from 1928-33. He recalled four adult

The gathering of the Bonathan family to mark the 100th birthday of Mrs Elizabeth Bonathan on 14 October 1951.
(Original photograph kindly lent by Mr and Mrs R. Gill.).

Bonathans at that time, named by him as: Bill, Lew, Fern, and Eddy, and four boys: Cliff, Roy, Stan, and Herbert. I have been told more about the family by Mrs Gwendoline Gill (nee Bonathan) who recalled the 100th birthday of her grandmother, Mrs Elizabeth Bonathan, on 14 October 1951, which was marked by a large family gathering in Buckfastleigh. The Parochial Church Council sent the centenarian Mrs Bonathan a card of congratulations and good wishes. (Mrs Gill and her husband, Reginald, both of whom remember the church from their childhood years, and also their working days in the mill, were married at Holy Trinity on 5 August 1933). Another stalwart choir member whom I well recall was Mr Henry Foster; he and his wife kept a popular sweet shop (previously Canns') near Weech Corner. Wilf Joint related the episode which brought to an end his own time in the choir. When Wilf was aged fourteen and his voice changing Mr Penny decided to let him sing as an alto.

This necessitated him sitting near the red organ starter button. During one Friday evening practice the tedium became too much for Wilf. After eying the button for some time he gave way to temptation and pressed it, causing the organ to groan to a stop. Everyone giggled except - understandably - Mr Penny. Wilf had to admit what he had done, and was summarily told that his services would no longer be required.

During the incumbency of Mr Timms women and girls were allowed to join the choir, and Mrs Lucy Full was one who became a member at this time, joined by her sons and later her grandson Richard. Young members of the Billing family were also among the choristers. In the 1990s Mr John Gill completed a notable fifty years of membership of the choir, which was marked by the award of the long service medal of the Royal School of Church Music. Another medal of the RSCM, awarded to him in his earlier years, was in the church on the night of the fire, but miraculously sur-

The church choir with the Rev. J.W. Timms at the retirement of Mr Budden as organist on 1 October 1978.

vived the inferno and is now, somewhat charred, back in Mr Gill's possession. The choir in 1995 was smaller than previously, with men, women, and girls, but sadly no boys.

Buckfastleigh has for long had an energetic team of ringers. In recent past years these have included: Mr R. Locke, Mr C. Wilton, Mr J. Willard, Mr A. Lee, Mrs A. Lee, Mr K. Thomas, Mr P. Grute, Mr A. Reed, Mr P. Axford, Miss H. Voisey, Mr J. Jones, and Miss S. Grute, and there have been many others whose services have been greatly valued. The captain of the ringers is Mr J. Jones, with Mrs Jones vice-captain and secretary, and their two sons J.W. and J.K. Jones both members of the team. Others are Mr R. Crocker, Mr A. Barrow, and Mrs M. Riley. During the time of the Buckfastleigh bells' silence the ringers kept in practice by assisting in ringing at Buckfast Abbey. Such is the fraternal spirit between towers that Holy Trinity ringers are confident that help will be forthcoming from the Abbey, or from parishes such as Rattery, if after their period of difficulty they sometimes need to call on one or two ringers from elsewhere to help work the full peal of eight.

The reverent atmosphere in the church and the smooth running of services owed much to the quiet dedication and efficiency of the churchwardens and sidesmen. For me - as for many - attendance was quite a family affair, with my grandfather John William Warren a warden during my childhood, followed by my maternal uncle William Edward (Eddie) Coulton. His co-warden was a life-long friend of my father and family, Richard Tooley Willcocks ('Uncle Dick' to me). My grandfather had become a churchwarden in 1919, joining Mr Philip Jackson, who was also vice-chairman of the newly formed Parochial Church Council. By around 1930 Mr John Rowland had become warden in the place of Mr Jackson, and he and my grandfather continued through that decade. Both died, within a

short time of each other, in 1940 (and, by coincidence, both their widows - my grandmother and Mrs Susan Rowland - later also died in the same year - 1955 - with only ten days separating the dates). Their successors held office together until 1965, when Mr Coulton retired and his place was taken by Mr P.J. Jackson, who was joined in the following year, on Mr Willcocks' retirement, by Mr E. Midgley. In 1978, Mr E. Scoble was warden in the place of Mr Midgley and served for three years. The following year Mr Jackson retired and Mr J.H.P. Berry was elected. Sadly, Mr Berry died in the same year; in 1980 Lt. Commander N.M. Walker was chosen to fill the vacancy, and he was joined in office in 1981 by his predecessor's widow, Mrs Elizabeth Berry. Mrs Berry continued as churchwarden through to 1993, in company first with Mr G.J. Gill (1983-89), and then with Commander Ivor Thorning (1989-93). In 1993 they were replaced by Mr Michael Ansell and Mrs Rhoda Look (a descendant of the Jacksons). Mr Ansell resigned in October 1994 and his place was filled by Mr Peter Kennett.

The verger and sexton at Holy Trinity from 1915 to 1936 was Mr George White (who was also the town crier), followed by Mr W. Boyer. Mr R. Locke has undertaken such work in recent years.

Buckfastleigh has also had an active and effective Parochial Church Council. Its secretary in the early 1920s was Mr Robert Jackson, who was followed by the Revd L. Illingworth Butler from 1922-3, and Mr J.R. Bartle for a spell from 1924. During the 1930s the secretary was Mr H.J. Jeffrey, the local school headmaster, who also, as I remember, read the lessons in church. In 1939, on moving to Totnes, he was succeeded in all three functions by Mr Kenneth Badman. In March 1942 pressure of work caused Mr Badman to resign as secretary and my aunt, Edith Warren (later Walters) was elected in his place. She carried out the work for forty-six years, resigning in 1988 at the age of ninety-three. (Mr Badman's successor as headmaster, Mr A. W. Thompson, also followed him as lesson reader in church). Subsequent secretaries have been : Mr Jack Knowling (1988-92), Mrs Joan Winson (1992-3), Mrs Julie Soul (1993-6), and Mrs Sharon Giles from 1996.

The church has had a number of associated groups. The Sunday School was long established, formerly held in the National School and faithfully served by a long succession of teachers, among them - years ago - the Misses Mabel and Violet Hamlyn, Miss Chaffe, Mrs H. Foster, and Mr W. Lane. My aunt Edith Warren (Walters) after starting as a pupil went on to teach in the Sunday School for most of her life. Latterly the Sunday School was taken on by the Revd Eric Jones, followed by Mr Jack Lee and then Mrs Lee, but sadly it does not function at present.

Both my grandmothers were members of the Mothers' Union, which was often, in the past, run by the vicar's wife. The enrolling member is currently Mrs Peggy Henley. There were also District Visitors, for whom Mrs Churchward was an organiser, and distributors of the parish magazine.

In times past annual outings and 'treats' were of great importance in parish life, and involved considerable numbers. The Sunday School treat was hugely supported - a typical example was on 6 July 1949 when 300 boarded a special train for a day at Teignmouth. Wilf Joint recalled how in the 1930s the scholars would march to the station with buckets and spades, each clutching the shilling spending money given to them, wearing new sandshoes (plimsolls) and clean underwear 'in case something happened '. The second annual highlight for the Sunday School

A day out, possibly a Mothers' Union group, around 1930. At the rear of the charabanc is the Rev. H. Mylchreest with his wife beside him. The author's grandmother, Mrs Warren, is in the group standing (second from left).

A charabanc trip in the late 1920s. The group includes the author's grandfathers E.J. Coulton, in the rear seat wearing a white hat, and J.W. Warren standing tall next to him. The author's father is in the front seat sitting next to the driver, Fernley Millman.

remembered by Wilf was the annual prizegiving held early in the year, in the National School upper room. After some words from the vicar, from the lady superintendent (Mrs Foster), and the superintendent of the boys (Mr Lane) the prizes were distributed - all of them good books with suitably inscribed plates, the result of donations. Afterwards, as the children filed out each one was given a large currant bun and an orange.

There were also day trips for the various organisations, by charabanc. These 'charas' were usually without a central passageway, as coaches have now, but consisted of rows of seats, each with a separate door, with a canvas hood that could be folded back for open travelling. Usually a coastal resort - in south or north Devon, or perhaps even in Dorset or Cornwall, and sometimes involving a drive across Dartmoor - would be the objective. The choir, the ringers, and the Mothers' Union all had outings of this kind. Annual

bazaars, for money raising, were other notable features of the church's year.

At Buckfastleigh the dividing line between church and secular activities has always been slight, and the town was notable for great community spirit. Certain philanthropic and friendly associations have existed in the town, which have involved church people as well as those from other denominations, who have worked happily together. These included a Nursing Association to support a nurse for the community, in which both my grandmothers were active. One of the later, practical, developments in this direction has been the conversion of part of St Luke's Church as a social centre, and particularly as a day centre for elderly and infirm people. There are now groups and activities for almost all ages of the population, from Toddlers' Playgroup to Age Concern. For the Royal British Legion the annual Remembrance Day service

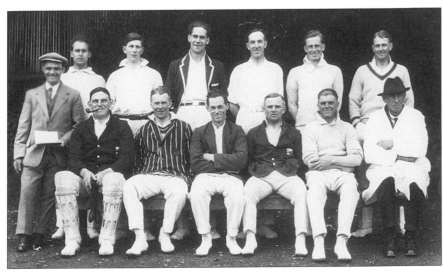

Buckfastleigh Cricket Club c. 1930. The author's father is seated, second from left.

in the Parish Church and the ceremony at the war memorial have always been an important date in the calendar. The town's Women's Institute has existed since 1946, and another long-established organisation is the Buckfastleigh Amateur Dramatic Group, which was started during the Second World War and has continued to delight audiences with regular productions ever since.

A feature of the hill on which the church stands, which was initially of interest mainly to local people but is now widely known and scientifically recognised, is the system of limestone caves. The late Wilf Joint together with Mr Edgar Reed explored these in the 1930s, and made notable discoveries of three previously unknown caves, in which were found bones of animals long here extinct.[3] Interest in the caves, and the bats which inhabit them, grew steadily. The land beneath which they exist belonged to my mother's family, the Coultons, from whom, in a sale of 1961, it was bought by the Society for the Preservation of Nature Reserves. Subsequently the William Pengelly Cave Studies Centre was established in Russets Lane in

1962 as a focus for cave studies and conservation. The Joint-Mitnor cave is of special interest, with its animal remains from around 100,000 years ago. The caves are frequent haunts of members of Devon Speleological Society, whose explorations at times bring them directly beneath the church's structure.

Sport and games of various kinds have for long been a cherished part of Buckfastleigh life - often participated in by the clergy as well as by parishioners. Buckfastleigh Rugby Club and Rangers Association Football Club (for which my father played in the 1920s) were both established many years ago. My father was also a regular member of Buckfastleigh Cricket Club (established in the 1860s)[4] through the 1920s and '30s, and I often went up to the Recreation Ground near the road to Holne, with my mother and grandparents to watch. Many of the players of these games on Saturdays have also been church members, and often points concerning the previous day's play would be discussed in church, in whispers behind cupped hands, before the Sunday morning service began.

Another game that has become increasingly popular over recent years, bringing together church members and others, is bowls. The Buckfastleigh Bowling Club, for all ages and both sexes, during the season plays two matches a week as members of the mid-Devon league. Bowlers and also tennis players use the Hamlyn Playing Field close to Little Bossell Lane.

It is probably true to say that, earlier in this century, most of the Buckfastleigh parishioners - even devout church people - if asked what happened at Whitsun, would not immediately respond with reference to Pentecost and the festival of the Holy Spirit, but would quickly reply: 'The Races'. The Buckfastleigh Hurdle Races and Steeplechases, held under National Hunt Rules, were indeed notable events for people in the locality, and attracted large numbers from other parts of Devon and of the country. My family on the Coulton side were greatly involved in running the meetings, which originated in the nineteenth century.

On 6 July 1861 the *Totnes Times* advertised 'A Steeplechase. 1st and 2nd August at Wallaford Down. Clerk of the Course Mr Richard Barter of Buckfastleigh'. A year later, on 19 July 1862 there was a similar advert, this time for 7 and 8 August, but whether or not the races continued thus in all the immediately successive years is uncertain. However, in 1883 it was decided at a meeting, at which Mr John Callard (flour and coal merchant of West Mill) was elected chairman and honorary secretary, to introduce hurdle racing. The first meeting in this form was held on 3 August that year, moved at this time to Dean Marshes, on the land of Dean Court in neighbouring Dean Prior parish farmed by my great-grandfather William Richard Coulton. In 1886 the event was first held on Whit Monday, and this became established as the traditional date. (An exception was in 1910, when the meeting was transferred to Saturday 21 May, on account of the recent death of King Edward VII which necessitated some alterations in dates of subsequent events). The races were discontinued in wartime, but in 1921 the fixture was extended to a second day, on the Tuesday, and in 1937 a third day - the Saturday following the first Monday in August - was added. When, after the Second World War, the races were resumed in 1946, this Whit Tuesday meeting was transferred to the preceding Saturday. In the late 1950s further race days were held, on the last Saturday in August and one in April, making five in all.

My maternal grandfather, Edward James Coulton, was largely responsible for the early success and development of the meeting. He rode a horse called Wild Rose on the first day in 1883 at Dean Marshes and was associated with the arrangements before becoming honorary secretary in 1906. In 1912 he also became clerk of the course and held both offices until his death in 1934. Later the races became an increasingly family affair with Mr Coulton's sons Edward (Buckfastleigh's later churchwarden) becoming stakeholder; John, clerk of the course; and Guy, honorary secretary. Their respective sons were also members of the committee as was my father J.R.H. (Jack) Warren - their brother-in-law - who also acted as clerk of the scales.

From my early years I felt a part of this family tradition and was aware of the amount of work that went on behind the scenes. Before the war the strings of racehorses arived at Buckfastleigh Railway Station and many of them would be led up to allocated stables in the town. This was a 'curtain raiser' for Buckfastleigh people, a few of whom would be hosting an equine guest - usually much favoured in the running. Later further stables were constructed at Dean Court and most horses arrived in large well-appointed horseboxes. Although many of the entries for the races were from local owners, horses would be brought to Buckfastleigh by the top trainers in the country- and ridden by leading jockeys. An extremely popular steward, owner and amateur rider at Buckfastleigh until his death in May

Racecard for Whit Monday 1906.

1950 was the former Hon. Anthony, later Lord Mildmay. Tall, pale, thin, and slightly stooping in his blue and white hooped colours, he was a familiar figure in the paddock before the race, and then, more often than not, the shouts would go up from the rails 'Come on, Lordy' as he chased past the post. He was believed to have been responsible for interesting Princess Margaret in Buckfastleigh Races; Her Royal Highness attended the Whit Monday meeting of 6 June 1949, which helped to bring attendance figures on that day to 23,000. Usually crowds at this time

This page and facing page: two views of the races attended by Princess Margaret on 6 June 1949. Although the racecourse has long since closed, the grandstand remains as a familiar landmark to travellers on the A38 Expressway between Exeter and Plymouth. (Originally published by the *Western Morning News*, photographs kindly lent by Mrs A. Coulton.).

numbered between 12,000 and 14,000. The improvement in financial returns in the early post-war years made it possible for the committee to plough back profits and provide improved facilities for racegoers. Previously a large timber grandstand had been erected and dismantled each season on the hill overlooking the very attractive race-course, but now, to the pride and joy of the committee, a new, permanent stand was built. Besides those from Buckfastleigh who attended just as a 'day out' - frequently including the clergy and their families, and usually some Roman Catholic priests - many local people were enlisted for paid duties on the course, such as on the gates and turnstiles, and the employment was welcomed. Sadly, in 1960, National Hunt racing at Buckfastleigh came to an end. The land on which the races were held was sold by its owner, Lord Churston, and my uncle, John Coulton, tenant of Dean Court, decided to retire. This, combined with other circumstances, made continuation impracticable. The course was later used at times for point-to-point races, and forlorn remains of the grandstand still exist on the site.

These days, many people go farther afield for their leisure and recreations and in the opinion of a number of Buckfastleigh people, there is less community spirit than in the past. Perhaps this is inevitable in the modern age. But one may hope that, as life changes, and new features become developed in the local scene, something will be remembered of Buckfastleigh in the days leading up to the present, and of those people - many more than have here been named - who have participated in, and contributed to its growth.

See page 95 for notes on Chapter 6.

❦ CONCLUSION ❦

So, what is to be the future for Holy Trinity Church, Buckfastleigh and this hallowed place where our Lord has been worshipped for possibly nearly half the time since he was on earth? Are we, the inheritors of all that has been built up through the faith and striving of our forbears over the centuries, just to let it all slide through our fingers?

The time following the disastrous fire saw an amount of apathy and negative thinking amongst individuals and bodies, in the parish and beyond. Such are the normal concomitants of shock and despair, and understandable in today's economic climate. The existence of St Luke's Church in the town led to ideas for abandoning the church on the hill as a sad ruin, perhaps with just a memorial tablet, in a Beeching-like act, and concentrating all worship in the one below. But, while all services have subsequently been held in St Luke's, with the secularisation of part of that building as a social centre (changes that probably would not have been made if the loss of Holy Trinity had been envisaged) many parishioners feel that services here do not entirely fulfil their spiritual needs and aspirations.

It may be remembered that, whilst Jesus did indeed come down to meet people at their point of need, he also knew the value of the sense of nearness to God to be found in high, quiet places. And, besides going to such places alone, he also gathered the crowds and preached to them up on the hills. Standing today on the Mount of the Beatitudes, beside the beautiful modern church, and looking out across Galilee to the distant Syrian hills, can evoke something of a similar sensation to that which may be felt when viewing from the tower of Holy Trinity Church the valleys and hills that rise to Dartmoor.

In these days, of cars with room for passenger lifts, and when people think nothing of walking miles for pleasure, is it too much to hope that local people may once more be glad to ascend the hill to worship on occasions at Holy Trinity? To take an example from across the moor, Brentor, now one of a group of parishes, still retains its ancient parish church 'on the tor', whilst having a Victorian church - used more often - in the village itself. Many travellers from places far afield visit Brentor church, as they do such other holy places as the abbey on remote Iona, and, indeed Buckfast Abbey. Buckfast is a striking example of the rebuilding, through faith, of an earlier church, to which very many people come. May the old parish church on the hill just above be accorded similar treatment, so that in the new millennium many of those who come to Buckfast may also make the brief ascent to that other place of worship, restored through faith, love and prayer, and with a proportion of new, inspired architecture?

During 1996, since completion of the repair work already described, progress has virtually come to a standstill. This is perhaps not surprising given the months of vacancy between vicars. While insurance money in respect of Holy Trinity, paid following the fire, rests in the bank together with various private donations, there is division of opinion in the parish as to whether this might be diverted to finance work on St Luke's. This view does not find favour with those who wish new life for the more ancient and historic building. Meanwhile, some parishioners appear despondent at repeated occasional acts of vandalism which the isolated situation of Holy Trinity seems to attract.

There are hopes that, under a new incumbent, fruitful discussions may take place and a suitable compromise be reached. Consideration will undoubtedly be given to the plan by Ronald Weekes for a roofed 'pilgrimage' chapel to be constructed within the walls, at the west end, with a glass screen dividing it from the east end, openable so that the whole area might be used for certain occasions - some services and perhaps also suitable musical events. Flexibility of use would be the aim, and the combination of antiquity and modern work would undoubtedly attract much interest.

As the church's isolation appears to cause problems of security, might there be some justification here for overriding current planning restrictions so as to provide a minimal degree of acceptable habitation in the vicinity of the church? This could offer a protective measure for the important building.

Despite the inevitably pervading air of sadness, those who have been involved in work on its structure, including young men, have appeared positive in their work. Care is still taken in trimming the churchyard grass. Can we find the ways and means to nurture those shoots of hope, and to ensure that there is a new restored future for the church on the hill?

ADDENDUM

2002 Update

Since the publication of this book in 1996 events concerning Buckfastleigh's church have taken a different turn from those anticipated. While the restored remains of Holy Trinity, on the hill, are preserved, and occasional services still held within the unroofed walls, views were expressed that the parish's main place of worship should be better sited within the actual town area. Following the fire, St Luke's Church, built as a 'chapel-of-ease' in the late nineteenth century, was used for all services, but considered inadequate to serve as the parish church in the longer term.

In 1997, therefore, a decision was taken to build a new church on the site of St Luke's which would address the needs of the community in the new millennium.

The former St Luke's was subsequently dismant and building of the new one, designed by archit Ronald Weekes, begun in June 2000. Of visiona. design, with ancillary features added as befit modern requirements, including a hall and meeting rooms, the church itself has been planned to seat 230, plus a further 100 by opening dividers to the lounge. Various features of the old St Luke's, including its stained glass window, are incorporated, and the ancient Norman font saved from Holy Trinity housed for continuing use within. Consecration is planned for 2002.

The church on the hill – for such it still is – continues as a place of pilgrimage for many, where a sense of peace, recollection, and inspirational outlook provides a cherished location for quiet prayer and contemplation.

H.H.

APPENDIX 1
THE VICARS OF BUCKFASTLEIGH

1. **Walvanus**, instituted 12 January 1263 or 64. Patrons, the Abbot and Convent of Buckfast. Died 29 March 1310. On his death,

2. **William de la Fenne**, inst 11 April 1310. Patrons the same.

3. **Thomas de la Fenne**, inst 6 February 1322 or 23. Patrons the same.

4. **John de Poghulle**, inst 16 May 1349. Patrons the same.

5. **William**, mentioned as vicar 1353.

6. **John de Brugge**, mentioned as vicar 1382. (Had previously been Vicar of Townstal).

7. **John Fardell**. His body was to be buried in Buckfastleigh church, near his parents. On his death,

8. **David Hugh**, inst 26 August 1406. Patrons the same. On his death,

9. **Roger Goslay**, inst 30 June 1414. Patrons the same. On his death,

10. **Richard Profete**, inst 2 December 1415. Patrons the same. On his resignation,

11. **Henry Baudyn**, inst 22 December 1416. Patrons the same. On his resignation,

12. **Walter Abbot**, inst 20 June 1433. Patrons the same. (He was ordered by the bishop to pay 8 marks a year to his predecessor).

13. **John Weryng**, inst 24 March 1473 or 74. Patrons the same.

14. **Nicholas Page**. Date of institution not known.

15. **Philip Phrer**, inst 8 December 1535. Patrons the same. (Vicar at the time of the Dissolution). (Post Reformation).

16. **George Carsleigh** (or Caseley), BA Oxon 1532, inst 25 July 1550. He was a schoolmaster. Patron John Tregonwell.

17. **Peter Langston**, inst 3 December 1573. Patron Queen Elizabeth I. On his death,

18. **John Dolbeare**, BA, inst 29 December 1609. Patron King James I. He matriculated at Exeter College, Oxford 1578 age 19, BA 1601-2. There were several Dolbeares living in Ashburton at this time.

19. **John Courtice**, BA, inst 13 December 1642. Patron Richard Cabell. He was the son of William Courtice of Bradwood (sic), Devon. The register records his burial 28 October 1672. On his death,

20. **Humphrey Sainthill**, MA, inst 19 December 1672. Patron Elizabeth, daughter of Richard Cabell. He was the son of Humphrey Sainthill, Rector of Zeal Monachorum, and matriculated at Exeter College, Oxford, 1650, BA 1656, MA 1658, Fellow 1653-62. He

married at Buckfastleigh, December 1674, Mary Terry, widow, of Dartington. Five of his children were baptised at Buckfastleigh: Samuel, Peter, Peter(2), Thomas and Humphrey. Samuel, Peter and Thomas all died in infancy. A small floor slab near the altar recorded the burial of Peter. The name of Sainthill is perpetuated in Jordan Street, at the location of the old vicarage; opposite was the tithe barn. He was buried at Buckfastleigh 23 December 1697. On his death,

21. **Thomas Escot**, inst 13 May 1698. Patron King William III.

22. **James Cornelius**, MA, inst 12 March 1700 or 1. Patrons Thomas Feock, Edward Cooke and ..... D'Oyley. The son of James Cornelius of Salisbury, matric Oxford 1691, BA 1694-5, MA 1697. On his resignation,

23. **Robert Bradford**, BA, inst 1717 or 18. Patron Richard Fownes, of Stapleton, Dorset. He was the son of John Bradford of Poughill. Matric Balliol, Oxford 1712, age 18, BA 1715, MA 1718. Registers record burial of three of his wives, the fourth survived him. He was buried 19 April 1777, his tomb under a yew tree. It is possible that an old silver porringer, once used as an alms dish, was presented to him. On his death,

24. **John Corham Huxham**, MA, inst 12 July 1777. Patron J. C. Huxham. The son of John Huxham, a doctor of Plymouth. Matric Exeter College, Oxford, 1740, BA 1743-4, MA 1746-7. He had previously been curate of Stoke Dameral, and was a Fellow of the Royal Society. His burial is not recorded in the register. On his death,

25. **Samuel Davenport**, inst 29 October 1778. Patron Sarah Huxham of Camberwell.

26. **Matthew Lowndes**, BA, inst 19 June 1782. Patrons Matthew Lowndes and Thomas Jephson of Camberwell. He was a Foundation Scholar of St John's, Cambridge, BA 1777. Buried 23 May 1825 age 73. On his death,

27. **Matthew Lowndes**, BA, inst 1 July 1825. Patrons Matthew Lowndes. the son of the late vicar. Educated at Merchant Taylors' School, matric Exeter College, Oxford 1804 age 17, BA 1810. Buried 9 June 1856 age 68. Memorial window in church. On his death,

28. **Edward Morland Chaplin**, MA, inst 20 August 1856. Patron Richard Champernowne of Dartington. Son of Edward Amos Chaplin of London. Matric Oxford 1850 age 18, BA 1854, MA 1856. Before coming to Buckfastleigh was curate of Harberton, later resigned for Rectory of Chilton, Berks, where he died 1877. On his resignation,

29. **John Jackson Manley**, MA, inst 22 January 1858. Patron the same. Eldest son of John Manley MD of Barking, Essex. Matric Oxford 1848 age 18, BA 1852, MA 1855. After leaving Buckfastleigh was Rector of Cottered, 1861-70. Died 1886, on his resignation,

30. **George Frederick Bullock**, MA, inst 26 June 1860. Patron the same. Fifth son of Edward Bullock of St Giles', London. Matric Oxford 1845, age 18, BA 1849, MA 1852. Curate of Widecombe-in-the-Moor 1858-9. After leaving Buckfastleigh was Curate of Torwood 1861-3, of St John's, Torquay 1863-6, of Bovey Tracey, and sub-Warden of the Devon House of Mercy 1866-81. Late curate of Rownhams, Hants, and Vicar of King's Sutton, Oxford 1886-1902. Died between 1906 and 1909. On his resignation,

31. **Matthew Lowndes**, BA, inst 30 October 1861.

Patron, Matthew Lowndes. Eldest son of Matthew Lowndes (no. 27). Matric Oxford 1856 age 21, BA 1859. On his resignation,

32. William Henry Browse Tucker, MA, inst 1 May 1891. Patron Mrs Tucker. Eldest son of William Edward Tucker of London. Matric Oxford 1870, age 19, BA 1873, MA 1876. Was Curate of Lower Broughton, Manchester, 1874-6, of Cheadle, Cheshire 1876-7, of Lancaster 1877-8, of St. Philip, Salford, 1878-84 and of High Lane, Cheshire 1884-91. Died 1907, buried in the churchyard. On his death,

33. Henry Frank Nesbitt, MA. Collated 18 August 1908. Patron the Bishop, by lapse. Only son of Francis Albert Nesbitt FRCS, of Wolverhampton. Westminster School 1878-80, Clare, Cambridge BA 1887, MA 1898. Curate of Ilfracombe 1892-1908. Vicar of Winkleigh 1918-25. Rector of St Paul with St Pancras and Allhallows, Goldsmith Street, Exeter, 1925. On his resignation,

34. Stainforth John Chadwick Lucas, BA, inst December 1918. Patron R.A.D. Fleming. Peterhouse, Cambridge, BA 1903. Previously Curate of Rowbarton, 1905-8, of Kirkley, Lowestoft, 1909-12, of Plympton St Mary 1912-18. Resigned 1929 to become Rector of East Allington. On his resignation,

35. Horace Mylchreest, L.Th. Durham, inst 27 May 1929. Patron the same. Curate of St Silas, Byker, 1911-13, of St Stephen, Elswick, 1913-15, of All Saints, Eastbourne, 1916-19, T.C.F. 1916-19, Curate of Cheam, 1919-20, Rector of Chedington, 1921-22, Rector of Thornbury 1922-29. Resignation from Buckfastleigh 1942 to become Rector of Berrynarbor.

36. John William Timms, MA, BD, inst 16 January 1943. BD University of London 1930, BA Oxford 1933, MA 1943. St Stephen's House, Oxford 1932. Ripon Hall, Oxford. Barnett School, 1954-55. Curate of St Paul, Finchley, 1933-6, Windlesham 1936-9, Rector of Combe-in-Teignhead 1939-43, Vicar of Buckfastleigh from 1943 (with Dean Prior from 1960) to 1981. Rural Dean of Totnes 1956-60. On his death,

37. Richard De Courcy Steele-Perkins, inst 1981. Patron the Revd. H. Mylchreest. Born 1936. Clifton Theological College 1961. Curate Stoke Gabriel 1964-5, Washfield 1965-8, Priest-in-Charge Wimbledon 1968-70, Assistant Chaplain St Thomas's Hospital, London, 1970-4, Chaplain Lambeth Hospital 1970-4, Priest-in-Charge Tawstock, and of Sticklepath, 1974-5, and incumbent of both 1975-81. Resigned 1990, to Midsomer Norton. On his resignation,

38. Paul Edward Wilson, inst 1991. Patron the Dean and Chapter of Exeter. Born 1943. Ridley Hall, Cambridge 1981. Curate Brightstone and Brooke with Mottistone, Portsmouth and Shorwell with Kingston 1983-6, Team Vicar Tring 1986-90, Priest-in-Charge Renhold and Chaplain HM Prison, Bedford 1990-1.

39. Derek John Rowland, inst 1996. Patron the Board of Patronage. Born 1947. London City Mission 1971-84 at St Mary's, West Kensington and Christ Church, Fulham. St John's College, Nottingham 1984-86. Ordained 1986. Curate St James, Porchester, Notts, 1986-89; Vicar St John the Divine, Fairfield, Liverpool, 1989-96.

The main source for this list is a set of handwritten notes prepared in March 1931 by the Revd Frank Nesbitt for Miss Hamlyn, for the purpose of a tablet showing the succession of vicars which she was to give to the church. Later in the year Mr Nesbitt returned to the parish, preached at the harvest festival services, and unveiled the tablet, which had been fixed to the wall in the church porch. The tablet survived the fire of 1992 and was rescued and taken into safe keeping by Mr John Gill. *Crockford's Clerical Directory* has been referred to for later entries.

Mr Nesbitt noted his sources of information as the registers of the church, transcribed, and the MS in the hands of Devon and Cornwall Record Society, Exeter. Also, he used notes from John Courtice (no. 19) to E.M. Chaplin (no. 28), in *Devon and Cornwall Notes and Queries* Vol XIII pp 75-81 (April 1924).

Later, in *Devon and Cornwall Notes and Queries* Vol XXIX (1962) Dom John Stephan, OSB, produced a similar list of vicars, acknowledged as being largely based on that prepared by Mr Nesbitt. He noted, however, that he had since discovered, on examination of Dean Milles' MSS, two names which had not appeared in the earlier list, but which were reckoned as benefactors of Buckfastleigh. They were, John Langfer (1610) and Christopher Furneaux (1642) both 'vicars of the church'. Exactly how they would have fitted into the list is not clear, but the supposition is that they may have resigned before their deaths and created a vacancy.

However, the late William Hamlyn, of Hapstead, in his history, *The Furneaux Family*, privately circulated in the 1930s, mentions that the Revd Christopher Furneaux, who graduated at Exeter College, Oxford, took Holy Orders and went to Buckfastleigh, probably as curate to the vicar, the Revd John Dolbeare, and married his only child Sybil there in 1625. They had six sons and four daughters, all registered at Buckfastleigh.

(It is of interest to me that the Revd John Dolbeare was my great x 8-grandfather, through both sides of my family. One of Christopher and Sybil's children, another Christopher married Mary Chaffe, and their great grand-daughter Mary married my ancestor John Warren, while their son Samuel Furneaux - who incidentally married an Ann Colton or Coulton - was a direct ancestor on my maternal grandmother's line. In view of the apparent evolution of the Warren surname it is tempting to wonder if the Revd John Weryng, No. 13, was also a forbear).

APPENDIX 2
NOTE ON BUCKFASTLEIGH CHURCHWARDENS' ACCOUNTS

The Buckfastleigh Churchwardens' Accounts, held in the Devon County Record Office, provide an interesting insight into parish affairs from the early years of the eighteenth century and into the nineteenth. As would be expected, they note sums paid for work done in the church, and for items used, such as nails, and glass for windows, for carrying materials including moorstone, timber, lime, water and clay, and also for agricultural products such as hay and dung - presumably for use on the glebe. Against these, receipts from rents of parish land are listed, together with income from the letting of seating in the church, and from other sources. It is interesting to read that in 1761 Thomas Hamlyn received £20 for a new pulpit, cannopie (sic) and stairs, and that in 1762 payment was made for 'taking down bell at vicarage'. There are numerous entries for washing surplices, or the 'surplis', which indicate that the wearing of this garment by the priest - a controversial issue at certain times in the Church's history - was the custom at Buckfastleigh. Also listed were the costs of bread and wine for the sacrament.

Besides payments connected with the bells, already referred to (page 44-46), there are entries for payments to the ringers on special occasions, including, in 1714, 'On Coronation Day' (evidently that of George I) 10 shillings. In 1783 a shilling was paid 'for a prayer of thanksgiving for the Victory over France', and in 1797 two shillings when 'Sir John Jervis gained the victory over the Spanish fleet'. The 1797 accounts show a shilling spent 'for thanksgiving for the King's happy Deliverance from Death by the hand of Margt. Nicholson who attempt to stab him'. (This would have referred to George III).

Charitable giving is also noted including, 1718, 'Gave a travelling woman and 2 young children 6d' and in 1744 'Gave to a disabled soldier 3d'. Almost as numerous as those of any other category are entries for the killing of bird and animal pests. Species listed include: fox, jay (one penny), rook, crow, magpie, fitch, polecat, wild cat, 'mattroll' (in King's Wood in one instance), badger, and hedgehog. Hedgehog killings were numerous, perhaps because they attracted payment of 4d, but one wonders at the need to expend such sums on destruction of this poor creature, whose beneficial characteristics surely outweigh any real or imagined harmful ones.

The accounts are of interest for the churchwardens' and other names that are included. For example, there are numerous references to all my four grandparents' families: Warren and Hoare, Coulton and Furneaux, and the same would undoubtedly be the case for many other people who live at, or have roots in Buckfastleigh.

⚜

Buckfastleigh Churchwardens' Accounts, 1712-1843, Devon Record Office 3639A/PW1 and PW2.

The destruction of vermin was a statutory requirement from 1532-33. See P.J. Dillon and E.L. Jones 'Trevor Falla's Vermin transcripts for Devon' *The Devon Historian* 33 (October 1986).

The particular species indicated by the term 'mattroll' is uncertain, and the word is not included in the list given in the Appendix to the Dillon and Jones article. However, it may have been a local term or corruption for 'martin or marten cat' - a pine marten.

APPENDIX 3
STAINED GLASS WINDOWS AND OTHER MEMORIALS

Fortuitously, in 1991, Mr Wilf Joint prepared in note form a terrier of the stained glass and other memorials in the church. Almost all of these were destroyed in the fire of 1992, and Mr Joint died a few months later. The following is a transcription of his notes, as they were collected and written down. (Details regarding the bells are omitted here as the information in included in the following Appendix).

STAINED GLASS

EAST WINDOWS - arched. 3 panelled, stone mullions: Birth, Death (crucifixion), Ascension.

TWO SMALL SANCTUARY WINDOWS - St John and St Luke.

SOUTH EAST WINDOW - 3 large panels: St Peter, Christ, St Paul.
Small stained panels above - Inscription: Jacob Powning OBITT MDCCCXLIII Requiescant in pace. A.J.F. Powning obitt MDCCCXLVIII.

SOUTH TRANSEPT WINDOW - 3 large panels with small stained panels above. Mrs Matthew Lowndes OB MDCCCXXV. Jesu Mercie. Margaretta Lowndes OB MDCCCXXII

BAPTISTRY (left) 3 panelled windows with 2 small panels above. Inscription:: To the Glory of God and in Memory of William Ellis who died July 5 1837 aged 32. St Luke 11.18. Jesu Mercie. (middle) 3 large panels and 2 small ones depicting the damsel is not dead but sleepeth, Mark 5. 39. Inscription: This window is erected by George Fleming in affectionate remembrance of Elizabeth Harriet Constance Fleming. Born 15 Jan 1861. Died 16 Jan 1864.

SOUTH AISLE - Two latticed windows, stone mullions. 3 panels with rounded tops.

WEST END - 3 large panels and 2 small ones. Inscription: In grateful memory of a devoted pastor and faithful friend, Matthew Lowndes. He was, during a period of thirty-one years the earnest minded vicar of this parish and through the intervening years this church was restored. He departed this life 2nd June 1850. LAUS DEO.

RINGING CHAMBER - 3 large panels, stone mullions, 2 small plain ones. St Bartholomew, St Philip, St Andrew. Inscription: Edward Bovey Lowndes, Edward Owen Lowndes, Jacob Matthew Lowndes.

WEST, NORTH WINDOW - 3 large panels, 2 small ones depicting Last Supper. Inscriptions: (middle) W. Christopher Furneaux, died 1794 Mary Furneaux his wife, died 1799. This window was erected to their memory by Jane Furneaux their grand daughter who died 1881. (right) John Honniwell died 1822. Joan Honniwell his wife died 1881.

NORTH AISLE - 2 windows each with 4 large latticed panels and 3 small ones. Stone mullions.

NORTH TRANSEPT (Organ) - 1) 3 large and 2 small, 2) 3 large and 3 small, 3) 2 large.

NORTH EAST WINDOWS - One with 3 large plain panels and 11 small decorated ones. Cross in the central panel. Holy Holy Holy, Lord God Almighty, which was and is and is to come.

The other: 3 large decorated panels and 11 small decorated ones. Stone mullions.

Inscriptions: (1) J.H. Furneaux Dec 29 1851, C.H. Furneaux Dec 4 1861. (2) C. Furneaux Nov 5 1811, J. Furneaux Dec 11 1838. (3) H. Furneaux Aug 13 1807, A. Furneaux Jan 23 1812

CHANCEL - 2 small windows: 1) St Matthew, 2) St Mark.

OTHER MEMORIALS AND FURNISHINGS

(The hagioscope (squint) in the north transept, and holy water niche in the baptistry are noted).

HIGH ALTAR - Wood. 16 carved wooden figures. Altar ornaments: 2 brass candlesticks, brass cross inscribed AMDG Anne Walker died April 10th 1892.

REREDOS - Wood. 12 Apostles.

PULPIT - eight-sided carved wood.

LECTERN - Brass eagle, book rest with Bible, inscribed: In memory, Edith Mary Tanner, Born Hawson Court 1880, died Prestbury Glos 1901.

FONT AND COVER. Norman, lead-lined, stone carved font. Wooden domed cover with dove on top. (The font originally stood on the four pillars currently attached to the sides).

SCREEN TO CHOIR VESTRY (West end of church) Modern.

TABLET ON WALL OUTSIDE WEST VESTRY - This tablet has been placed here to record with grateful appreciation the gift by Mr and Mrs R. E. Chuchward of the two new bells, the re-casting of the original six, the ringing chamber, choir vestry and oak screen. Dedicated by the Lord Bishop of Exeter 12.1.1935.

WOODEN TABLET IN RINGING CHAMBER - The six bells in the tower of this church were re-hung in an iron frame by Mr Henry Stokes and Son of Woodleigh in Sept 1910 and were rededicated by the Rev Frank Nesbitt, MA, Vicar, 17.12.1910. Churchwardens Mr Charles Hoare, Mr J. S. Trelawney. Ringers: Messrs W. Paul, J. Chaffe, W. Stancombe, J. Hayman, M. Abbot, S. Pinney, J. Stancombe, W. Saunders, S. Hoppins. Sexton J. Chaffe.

OIL PAINTING in gilt frame, on north wall - Taking Christ from the Cross.

OIL PAINTING in gilt frame, in vicar's vestry - depicting a lady.

PICTURE OF CHURCH in vicar's vestry.

LIST OF VICARS in porch.

FLOOR SLATE SLAB - Peter, son of Humphrey Sainthill. Clerk, buried here Jun 23 1682.

LARGE STONE ALTAR TOP at one time used as headstone. Inscription: Here lyeth the body of William Gilbert who was buried here 21st day February 1633. Here also lyeth the body of Peter Gilbert, son of William Gilbert who died 20th day of November A.D. 1691. Also here lyeth Katherine the wife of Peter Gilbert who died 16 day of July 1699 aged 84 years.

BAPTISTRY SLATE WALL SLAB - Erected to the Glory of God and in memory of John William Timms, beloved vicar of this parish 1943-1981, by the churchwardens and the PCC.

WEST WALL OF BAPTISTRY, WHITE MARBLE - Sacred to the memory of Rear Admiral Thomas White who died at Buckfast Abbey in this parish November 18th 1846 aged 77, And of Sophia his wife who died July 23rd 1846 aged 69. Also of their second son Edward Thomas White, Paymaster and Purser R.N. who died while on relief service at Castleton, Ireland, July 23rd 1847 aged 42, and of his children Caroline Julie Buttervant White aged 5 years and Edward Barry White aged 3 years. Erected by their affectionate family.

FLOOR SLAB, SOUTH AISLE, ADJACENT TO BAPTISTRY - Here lyeth the body of William Gilbert, son of Peter Gilbert of Buckfastleigh, who was buried the 22 day of January AD 1679.

WAR MEMORIAL - wood, on south wall. To those who died in the 1914-18 and 1939-45 wars.

WHITE MARBLE PLAQUE ON SLATE BACKGROUND - Sacred to the memory of Lewis Harris of ? , surgeon, who died after a short illness. Resigned to the will of Heaven on the 15th day of September 1863 aged 23 years. His remains are interred in a vault in the churchyard. This monument is erected by an affectionate parent as a tribute of love.

WALL PLAQUE - Sacred to the memory of Th. Christopher Furneaux of this parish who died November 5 1811 aged 49 years, and of Mrs Furneaux

his widow also died December 11 1838 aged 62, also of Thomas William Ellis of Addislade in the parish of Dean Prior their son-in-law who died July 5 1837 aged 32 years.

WALL PLAQUE - sacred to the memory of Mr Robert Mitchelmore of Merryfield in this parish who died on 1st April 1826 aged 87 years, also of Grace Mitchelmore his wife who died on 26th February 1792 aged 48 years. Also of John Bovey Esq of Peartree in the parish of Ashburton who died on 15th November 1834 aged 63. Also of Mary Bovey his wife also died on 3rd November 1832 aged 58. Also of Edward Bovey their son who died on 27th January 1828 aged 25.

IN SAFE IN VICAR'S VESTRY - Communion set: flagon, chalice, paten, and wafer box and cloth in wooden box, given in memory of John William Warren, by his family. Set consisting of chalice, paten, flagon, in memory of W.H. Browse Tucker. Water flagon, waferbox, presentation tray. Very large flagon, gift of Mrs Joan Gould to the Church of Buckfastleigh 1786. In chest: alms plate (brass), alms plate (copper).

⚜

Since the 1992 fire two memorials and a wall panel were rescued and stabilised by Alison Hooper, conservator at Exeter Museum at the instigation of the Dartmoor National Park Authority, which arranged for the work to be carried out. These were memorials to members of the White and Gilbert families and an eighteenth century shield-shaped panel. Also Deborah Griffiths, Dartmoor National Park Archaeologist, has identified a reused gravestone of Cabell from the floor of the crossing.

APPENDIX 4
THE BELLS

The inscriptions on the bells, as recorded in 1935*, are as follows:

Treble Rev Matthew Lowndes, Vicar, Thos Bilbie, fecit 1794. Mr Samuel Furneaux and Mr Robert Webber, Ch Wardens.

Second When I begin let all strike in. T.B.fecit 1793. S.F. and R.W. Ch W.

Third Fear God honour the King. T.Bilbie, Cullompton, fecit. M.L. Vicar. S.F. and R.W. Ch Wardens. 1793.

Fourth Thomas Furneaux, Church Warden. W.B. Hambling, founder, Blackawton. 1844.

Fifth Keep Peace and Good Neighbourhood. M.L.Vicar. Mr S.F. and Mr R. W., Ch Wardens, T. Bilbie fecit 1793.

Tenor Religion, Death and Pleasure cause us to Ring. Thomas Bilbie, Cullompton, F. The Revd Matthew Lowndes, Vicar, Mr Samuel Furneaux and Mr Robert Webber Ch W 1793.

And the two new bells:

Treble "To the Glory of God" This bell was given by Mr and Mrs R.E. Churchward, 1934. "I lead" Audite et Venite.

Second "To the glory of God" this bell was given by Mr and Mrs R. E. Churchward, 1934. "I follow" Venite et Audite.
A further inscription was added on the Tenor: 'The six bells of this tower were re-cast and two new treble bells added through the generosity of Mr and Mrs R.E. Churchward 1934. H.M. Vicar, J.W.W. and W.J.R. Ch Wardens, H.J.J. Sec., PCC'.
The bells are tuned to the key of F Major. The weight of the largest bell is 15 cwt. 3 qr. 14 lb.

*The *Western Guardian*. 17 January 1935.

APPENDIX 5
THE WAR MEMORIAL

To the Glory of God
and in memory of
The Men of Buckfastleigh
who made the supreme sacrifice
in the Great European War
1914 - 1918
and in the Second World War
1939 - 1945
'Blessed are the dead who die in the Lord'
Revelations XIV 13

1914 - 1918

A.R.Addems	Jas Burge	W.H.Hayman	S.J.Pinney
H.Andrews	J.H.Burt	F.J.Hocking	H.Revell
S.Ash	R.Butland	D.E.C.Ireland	H.S.Sampson
W.R.Back	R.F.Coombes	E.H.Jones	A.Shute
T.H.Barnes	C.L.Divine	S.H.Kerswell	J.Symons
F.Bartle	F.Foster	F.C.P.Lock	E.L.Tooley
G.H.Beer	E.J.Foster	G.H.Loram	H.A.Tooley
S.J.Beer	E.R.Friend	C.S.Marks	A.Turner
H.Bickle	L.G. Furneaux MM	W.McCarthy	R.V.Walters
W.H.Bickle	E.Gidley	W.A.Norrish	T.Ware
A.H.Bonathan	G.L.Gill	S.Oxenham	H.Watts
G.Bowerman	F.Hare	G.A.Peardon	L.White

E.G.Hare   T.Polkinghorne

1939 - 1945

R.Arscott	R.B.Fleming	A.C.Smailes
S.Abbott	R.E.Perry-Hook	A.V.Tapper
L.C.Bonathan	D.W.Lane	M.G.Turner
R. Boon	G.E.Locke	S.Waye
P.N.Butler	J.H.F.Moat	E.H.Weeks
G.E.Castle	B.C.Parsons	A.Williams
W.G.Chaffe	D.J.Pulford	W.N.C.Woolacott
D.C.Coulton	W.J.H.Rice	H.Waters
J.Downie	H.Smailes	J.F.O.Yateman

A.H.N.D.Prendergast MC

APPENDIX 6
ARCHITECTURAL DESCRIPTION OF THE
PARISH CHURCH AND CHURCHYARD

Holy Trinity church together with the Cabell tomb and the chapel ruins in the churchyard were included on the statutory "list of buildings of special architectural or historic interest" under the Town and Country Planning legislation on 10th January 1951. Their listed status was confirmed when the list was revised in January 1983 and the Department of National Heritage issued a further revised list in December 1993. Although issued after the 1992 church fire, this new list was prepared from a survey carried out with the support of the Dartmoor National Park Authority in 1991/92 when the church was still intact. The detailed architectural description contained in the 1993 listing serves therefore as a final record of the church. It read as follows:

PARISH CHURCH OF HOLY TRINITY
GRADE II*

Parish church. Spectacularly sited on a high hill and some distance from the town below. C13 tower; chancel and transepts possibly also C13 in origin; C15 aisles and chancel chapels. Thorough restoration of 1844-45 to the designs of John Hayward of Exeter included new roofs and the upper part of the spire; severely damaged by fire on the 20th of July, 1992. Smooth cement-rendered (probably C19), the tower with earlier roughcast (spire also roughcast); granite dressings; purple natural slate C19 roofs with crested ridge tiles (except chancel); cast-iron rainwater goods with Art Nouveau design on the hopppers.
Plan: nave; chancel; W tower; N and S chancel chapels; N and S transepts, N used as organ chamber; 4-bay lean-to aisles; S porch; vestry to centre N.

EXTERIOR: C19 in texture and detail; most of the window mullions appear to have been renewed, several are variants on the uncusped design with round-headed sub-arches, possibly early C18 in date (cf Kelly parish church). The chancel, lower roof than the nave, has a coped gable with a big C19 foliated cross; 3-light Early English style E window with pointed uncusped sub-arches; 2 small chamfered lancets to N and S sides. S side has a probably C13 Early English hollow-chamfered doorway predating the chancel chapel with a probably C16 plank and studded door with a central cover strap over the hinges. 3 windows in the nave gable; 3-light in the centre with uncusped sub-arches, flanked by roundels. S chancel chapel has set-back buttresses with granite set-offs and an embattled parapet; E and S 3-light Perpendicular style traceried windows. N chancel chapel with plain parapet rising as gable to the east. E and N windows similar to S chapel but N window with crude replaced mullions; octagonal C15 rood loft stair turret abuts N chancel chapel on N side. S transept has E and S 3-light windows with round-headed uncusped lights. N transept has a square-headed 2-light E window, probably C16 in origin with cusped lights. High-set Georgian 2-light arched timber N window with intersecting glazing bars, probably to light a former gallery.
   N aisle has 2 unusual 4-light windows with depressed 4-centred arched heads, uncusped round-headed lights and a small round-headed light in the apex. N vestry has 3-light E window with round-headed uncusped lights. S aisle has two 3-light square-headed uncusped lights. S aisle has two 3-light square-headed windows (heads renewed) with round-headed lights and rustic carving in the spandrels; W window of 3 plain round-headed lights.

3-stage W tower with no string-courses or pinnacles. Shallow set-back buttresses and a plain corbelled parapet give an effect of vertical panels to each face. 5-sided N stair turret with an embattled parapet and slit windows. W face has a hollow-chamfered arched doorway with a C19 or C20 W door; 3-light Early English style W window with uncusped sub-arches. 2-light square-headed belfry windows to W and S faces with tre-foil headed lights; long slit window to S face. Somewhat irregular spure dating from Hayward's restoration.

South porch has plain arched outer doorway with c1840s 2-leaf door with flush panels below the middle rail and slats above. Inside, the porch has a 2-bay 1844 roof matching the nave and chancel, stone benches and a double-chamfered medieval inner doorway with ribbed stops. 2-leaf late C18/early C19 panelled inner door.

INTERIOR: plastered walls. Arcades with octagonal piers with double hollow-chamfered arches and capitals; similar arches into chancel chapels from the aisles and chancel. 2 of the N aisle piers are monoliths and may be C19. Very tall, narrow plain tower arch. Wide, double hollow-chamfered chancel arch on moulded granite corbels which do not match one another. Roofs of the 1840s by Hayward: 8-bay arch-braced nave roof with a ridgeboard and 2 tiers of windbraces; similar 2-bay transept roofs; unceiled lean-to aisle roofs might post-date Hayward's work. Blocked C15 doorway to rood loft stair. Plain arched sedilia; aumbry and piscina in the chancel, probably to Hayward's designs.

Fittings: fine Norman font re-sited in the S transept with a carved freestone bowl with some remains of colouring on its original cylindrical stem with 4 added shafts. Probably late C18 domed font cover. Late C19 timber drum pulpit with blind tracery decoration. Fine set of box pews, mostly of 1844 with blind trac-

eried doors, one painted with 'reserved for ringers'. The W end pews are probably earlier with panelled doors and are banked up to the W end. Chancel with C19 brass communion rail with foliage decoration and C20 choir stalls.

Memorials: two C17 slate slabs set into the floor, one in the chancel and one in the S transept.

Stained glass: an interesting set, mostly by Beer of Exeter, the E window of the S chancel chapel probably by Beer and Driffield. Unfortunately the backgrounds of several of the windows have been removed, leaving the figures isolated. S window of the S transept by Powell and Son, designed HE Wooldridge (Pevsner).

An early medieval church. The 1844-45 restoration and the Beer stained glass represent an unusual combination of local architect and craftsman.

The undated and unsigned architect's drawing in the porch shows the proposal to re-site the font in the S transept.

Historical note: John Hayward of Exeter was the leading local Gothic Revival church architect in the Exeter diocese in the 1840s and 1850s.

(Buildings of England: Pevsner N: Devon: London: 1989-: 226).

CHAPEL RUINS TO EAST OF
CHURCH OF HOLY TRINITY
GRADE II*

Chapel, possibly detached chantry chapel. Ruinous. c1300. Local grey slatestone rubble with freestone dressings. Plan: roofless ruin of an aisleless building of which the E wall, part of the S wall and a small section of the N wall remain.

EXTERIOR: very thick walls with putlock holes and a wide, deeply splayed E window, dressed externally with alternating bands of chamfered red and cream stone with a glazing rebate. The surviving dressings suggest a trefoil-headed window. The S side retains the remains of a similarily-decorated probably lancet to the E, the sill mended with mullions; a doorway with a cranked relieving arch (dressings gone) and the E jamb of another window. The N side preserves the fragmentary remains of the E jamb of another window.

INTERIOR: preserves the fragmentary remains of wall plaster. Close inspection reveals some traces of red and yellow painted decoration on the splay of the W window. A very unusual survival.

CHURCHYARD WALL INCLUDING LYCH GATE AND STILES TO SW OF CHURCH OF HOLY TRINITY
GRADE II

Churchyard walls to S and SW side of the churchyard including a lychgate and 2 stiles. Walls probably medieval; stiles C19, lych gate early C19 in origin, restored 1971 according to a plaque. Local grey slate-stone rubble; lych gate with slate roof and timber gates. Plan: the walls bound the churchyard on the S and SW sides. The S stile is connected to a steep path up from the town which begins as a long flight of steps (qv Station Road). Lych gate to the SW, fronting the road access from the town with a second stile to its E. The rubble walls are topped by a Devon hedgebank. The stiles each have large, irregular rounded standards with a single slab of slatestone between. Unusual lych gate design. 2 widely-spaced square section piers at either end are surmounted with pyramidal finials. Slate roof between, with a plastered soffit. A pair of gates in the centre are hung off moulded timber posts which extend to the roof of the lych gate. Pedestrian gate to the left; section of fencing to the right. The gates and fencing are of simple design with plain splat verticals with a slender central ledge, the main standards with shaped finials. Included for group value with the Church of Holy Trinity (qv), which is sited on a hilltop above the town.

CABELL CHEST TOMB AND STRUCTURE OVER TOMB TO S OF CHURCH OF HOLY TRINITY
GRADE II

Chest tomb in small rectangular building. c1656, commemorating Richard and Susanna Cabell (d. 1612 and 1597) and Richard, son of the above, d.1655 (Djabri). Mythology has it that the tomb is that of wicked Richard Cabell, d.1677 (Baring-Gould). Building appears to be partly Edwardian, or at least re-roofed in that period, although it is mentioned in 1879 (White). Freestone chest tomb: enclosed building cement-rendered and blocked out with a hipped slate roof.

Plan: sited just S of the church porch. The building has a doorway on the S side.

EXTERIOR: the building has a projecting stone plinth which functions as a seat. Chamfered granite corner posts rise form the plinth; roof with very deep coved eaves with plastered coving. Locked plank door on the S side; north side has a Victorian or Edwardian cast-iron grille with ornamental standards allowing a view of the chest tomb inside. Tomb rather damaged with a rubble chest with an oversailing chamfered freestone lid. An inscription (not legible through the grille) is carved in good Roman lettering on the chamfer with the word RICU on the edge of the lid on the S side. Historical note: local mythology, according to Baring-Gould, folklorist and novelist, reports that Cabell, of Brook Manor (West Buckfastleigh CP) died "with such an evil reputation that he was placed under a heavy stone and a sort of pent-house was built over that with iron gratings to it to prevent his coming up and haunting the neighbourhood. When he died .... fiends and black dogs breathing fire race over Dartmoor and surrounded Brooke, howling". The story is supposed to have been one which inspired Sir Arthur Conan Doyle to write The Hound of the

Baskervilles. By 1932 the building was known locally as 'The Sepulchre' and Cabell was reputed to gnaw the fingers of anyone who ventured to insert them in the keyhole (Nesbitt).

Susan Cabell Djabri has written a monograph debunking the myth and suggesting ways in which it might have developed. She argues that the 3rd Richard Cabell, who erected Brook Manor, erected this tomb for his father and grandparents. There used to be a weathervane, dated 1656, on top of the building over the tomb.

(Djabri S: *The Story of the Sepulchre*: London (private): 1960-; Methuen's Little Guides: Baring-Gould S: *Devonshire*: London: 1907-).

HAMLYN MEMORIAL APPROXIMATELY 44M SOUTH-WEST OF TOWER OF CHURCH OF HOLY TRINITY
GRADE II

Memorial to Joseph Hamlyn, d. 1864 and other members of the Hamlyn family. c1864. Polished and unpolished granite; cast-iron railings. Greek Revival style. Plan: pedestal monument enclosed by contemporary cast-iron railings.

EXTERIOR: pedestal gabled on all 4 sides with a draped urn on top. Moulded base and plinth, sides decorated with inscription shields with curled upper corners. Corbelled gables with friezes of decoration including Greek key pattern, gables decorated with sacred monograms. Surrounding cast-iron railings with cusped ogee and semi-circular rails with decorated finials and square section corner standards with moulded bases and finials. Historical note: the Hamlyn family were woollen mill owners in Buckfastleigh and responsible for building the town hall and extensive housing for their workforce in the town. One of the adjacent memorials (not included) is to the Callard family, also Buckfastleigh millowners.

STABLE AND CARRIAGE HOUSE IMMEDIATELY S OF LYCH GATE OF CHURCH OF HOLY TRINITY
GRADE II

Stable and carriage house, possibly designed for churchgoers, now partly used as tractor shed. Mid C19: not on the 1839 tithe map. Local stone rubble with a hipped slate roof. Plan: rectangular building sited close to the SW entrance to the churchyard. Carriage house at the right (NW) end with 2 stables to the left.

EXTERIOR: single-storey building with 2 doors to the left, a window alongside to the right and a gated open bay to the far right. The stable doors have ovolo-moulded and bolection moulded doorframes and stout plank doors with large iron drop latches. 2-light shuttered window with a bolection-moulded frame and 2-plank shutters with bead-moulded planks. Pretty timber carriage-house gate with a diagonal brace and splat verticals with shaped finials.

INTERIOR: carriage house has a plastered ceiling. Remainder not accessible at time of survey but might retain fittings of interest. Group value with the parish church (qv), which is sited on a steep hill some distance from the town, and must have required some provision for stabling during church services.

FLIGHT OF STEPS TO CHURCH OF HOLY TRINITY
GRADE II

Flight of stone steps leading from Station Road up the steep hill to the parish church, which stands above the town (qv). Probably C19 or earlier in origin, recently repaired. Rough limestone kerbs with pitched stone treads, laid in rough horizontal courses. About half way up the flight 2 adjacent steps have pitched stone treads laid at right angles to the others. These are known locally as the kissing steps. One step incorporates the initials TW, probably those of the repair mason. A distinctive and unusual feature in the town.

APPENDIX 7
RESIDENTS AND BUSINESSES OF BUCKFASTLEIGH
FROM KELLY'S DIRECTORY 1850

Angel Mr Thomas, *Fairies' Hall*
Barnes John, paper manfr. *Kilberley*
Barnes Mrs Sus. || Callard Mr John
Berry John, serge mfr. (& Ashburton)
Butchers John Carns, schoolmaster
Braine Mrs Mary, *Buckfast Abbey*
Chenhall James, watch maker
Class Rev John, (Independent,
Coates Mrs. *Brooke House*
Edwards Chas., Esq. *Coulson Grange*
Frogley Henry, druggist
Furneaux Christopher, maltster, &c
Furneaux John, insurance agent, &c
Furneaux Thomas, tailor
Gidley Mr Wm. || Hamlyn Jph.
Gover Mr Stephen, *Black Rock*
Hamlyn Brothers, tanners, wool-
  staplers, & serge manufacturers
Irish John & Rt. gents. *Hawson Clg*
King Richd. John, Esq. *Digailen Hs*
King Mrs Grace, and Miss Ann
Lowndes Rev Mattw., B.A., *Vicarage*
Mitchell John, tinner & ironmonger
Phillips Mrs Ann, *Crappin Park*
Savery Servington, Esq. *Hayford*
Symons John, cider merchant
Symons Thomas, woolstapler
Symons Mrs., *Road View House*
Trist R., Esq., *Milbrook House*
Tucker Mr Robert and Mrs
Vaughan Mrs. *Buckfast Cottage*
Warren John, woolstapler & spinner
FARMERS. (* are Owners.)
Barter Elias, *Scorraton*
*Barter Ann, *Runnaford Combe*
Barter John, *Warnacombe*
Berry Wm. *Abbey Grange*
Bowden Jeffery || Bowden James
*Callard Hy. (miller,) *West Mills*
Chaffe Roger, *Binaden*
Chaffe Robert, *Broom Parks*
Coates John, *Brook Farm*
Cruse Nicholas, *Buckfast*
Foster John, *Colston*
*Furneaux Samuel, *Button*
*Furneaux Saml. & John, *Hapstead*
Heath Thomas || Hendy Thomas
*Michelmore John, *Northwood*
*Petherbridge Richard, *Scorraton*
Petherbridge Wm. || Hodge Mr

Tooley Sus. || Scott Mr
Waycott Wm. || Wyatt Josias
INNS AND TAVERNS.
Commercial, Sus. Furneaux
Globe, George Cole
Golden Lion, John Churchward
Half Moon, John Hoarse
King's Arms, John Penny
Prince of Wales, Henry Choake
Royal Oak, Samuel Churchward
Sun, John Churchward
Town Arms, Henry Wilcock
Valiant Soldier, W. Foster
Waterman's Arms, Richd. Gibbins
White Hart, Thomas Petherbridge
BAKERS.
Chaffe Robert
Gibbins Richd.
Rice Wm.
Voce John
Wing Wm.
BLACKSMITHS.
Barter Richard
Boys Wm.
Easterbrook Jno.
Petherbridge Jas.
Prowse John
BUTCHERS.
Churchward Jas.
Holditch Robt.
Tooley John
Trist John
Trist Thomas
CARPENTERS, &c.
Abbott John
Adams John
Callard Thos.
March Adam
Pope Wm.
Prowse John, (&
  cooper)
Wilcocks John
LIME WORKS.
Coulton Wm.,
  Bully Clay
Furneaux Chas.,
  Baker Pits
MASONS.
Arscott John
Border John

Weeks Jas. & Jno.
Wilcocks Henry
PLUMBERS, &c.
Codd James
Yeo Doctor Dl.
SADDLERS.
Easterbrook Jas.
Thomas Agnes
SCHOOLS.
Bovey John
Butchers Jas. B.
  (and regr.)
SHOEMAKERS.
Border Thos.
Hannaford John
Lee Edward
Petherick Richd.,
  Buckfast
Tozer James
Tozer Wm.
Winter Wm.
SHOPKEEPER.
Arscott Eliz.
Bastow Wm.
Bishop Thos. dpr
Butchers Richd.
Coombe Eliz.
Easterbrook Jno.
Ezekiel Lionel
Petherbridge Wm
Shapter John
Treleaven Henry
  (and draper)
Warren Andw.
Warren Wm.

Preston James || Rouse Mr
Preston Richard, *Bowden*
Rowland Jacob, (miller,) *Brook*
Searell Wm. and Thomas, (millers)
*Symons Thomas, *Lovers Combe*

Churchward Jas.
Furneaux Seml.
Murch Thos.
Putt Thomas
Sincombe Peter

Wilcocks Eliz.
Wilcocks John
SURGEONS.
Evans James
Fisher Thomas

TAILORS.				POST OFFICE
Howell George	Bastow Wm.	Hunt John		At Wm. Foster's
Hayman John	Bunclark John	Lock John		CARRIERS to
Hayman Richd.	Churchward Jno.	Penny Thomas,		*Ashburton* daily,
Lee James	Codd Philip	Saml., & Geo.		and J. & T. Wil-
Warren Wm.	Cole John	Petherbridge Ts.		cocks to Totnes
WOOLCOMBERS.	Furneaux John	Shapter John		four times a
Arscott Wm.	Hamlyn Bros. (&	Warren John		week
Bastow Jno. Cole	manfrs)	Weeks Andrew		
	Howard Wm.	and John		

92

GENERAL SOURCES OF INFORMATION

Bibliography

Kelly's Directory of Devonshire 1850
White's Directory of Devonshire 1878
W.G.Hoskins, *Devon* Collins 1954, Devon Books 1991.
Helen Harris, *The Industrial Archaeology of Dartmoor* 1st edit.
David & Charles 1968, 4th edit. Peninsula Press 1992.
Nicholas Orme ed. *Unity and Variety* Exeter University 1991
Dom Adam Hamilton OSB, *A History of Buckfast Abbey* 1906
Dom John Stephan OSB, *A History of Buckfast Abbey* 1970
Joyce Youings, *The Dissolution of the Monasteries* 1971
Hilary Beard, *Buckfast in Bygone Days* Devon Books 1991
Robin Clutterbuck, *Buckfast Abbey a History* Buckfast Abbey
Trust 1994
Buckfastleigh and Buckfast Official Guide

Other sources

Westcountry Studies Library Parish File
Buckfastleigh Parochial Church Council minutes between
1920 and 1956
Various early copies of Buckfastleigh Parish Magazine
Miscellaneous notes from the collection of the late Mr W.
Joint
Diaries, notes, newspaper cuttings, old orders of service, and
received information from my late grandmothers, Harriette
Alice Warren (nee Hoare) and Helena Mary Coulton (nee
Furneaux), and mother, Helena Marianne Warren (nee
Coulton), and other family members.

SPECIFIC NOTES AND REFERENCES

Introduction (pages 5-6)
1. Helen Harris, *The Story of St Luke's* 1994

Chapter 1. The Parish of Buckfastleigh (pages 7-12)
1. For administrative purposes the parish is divided. In 1894
Buckfastleigh West became a civil parish separate from the
smaller urban area which had its own Urban District Council
first elected in 1895. The two are still separate, Buckfastleigh
West coming within the area of South Hams District
Council, and the former Urban area now in Teignbridge
District and having its own Town (parish) Council and
mayor.
2. Landscove, which borders the Dart here, has been a separate ecclesiastical parish within the civil parish of Staverton
since 1852.
3. See chapter on 'Dartmoor', by Helen Harris, in *The Duchy
of Cornwall* ed. Crispin Gill, David and Charles (1987).
4. For further information on archaeological features of the
moorland area of Buckfastleigh see Jeremy Butler, *Dartmoor
Atlas of Antiquities, Vol 4 the South-East*, Devon Books (1993).
5. 327 acres, including Hembury Castle, were given to the
National Trust by Mr Arthur Williams of Hockmoor House in
1947. Burchetts Wood was given to the National Trust in
memory of Mr Williams in 1960 by his niece Mrs E. M.
Dundas.
6. Helen Harris, *The Industrial Archaeology of Dartmoor* (1992)
p.189.
7. Jeremiah Milles, 'Parochial Returns' Bodleian Library MS
Top. Devon C.8 Microfilm copy in Westcountry Studies
Library, Exeter.
8. The black cattle were probably Devon Natts, a breed
believed to have been developed from stock introduced by
the Norsemen before the Norman Conquest, formerly found
in south Devon but long since extinct.
9. Bulley Cleaves Quarry was bought by my great-great-
great-grandfather Richard Coulton of Rock, Buckfastleigh, in
about 1851, from Mr Baring-Gould of Lewtrenchard, forbear
of the Revd Sabine Baring-Gould, rector and writer (including hymns). Apparently, accompanied by my great-grandfather, William Richard Coulton - who lived with his parents
at Dean Court - Mr Coulton rode across Dartmoor with he
money for the purchase in gold sovereigns, carried in his
saddle bag. They set out at 4.30am and after negotiating the
business, and having a meal, returned to Buckfastleigh the
same day. This Richard Coulton lived in a 'pretty cottage' at
Rock. It was his son who built the larger house, where my
grandmother lived in her widowhood until her death in
1958. It is now a residential home.

10. Robin Clutterbuck, *Buckfast Abbey a History* (1994) p.2.
11. Clutterbuck p.4.
12. Unidentified photocopy of ancient document from the W. Joint collection.
13. Clutterbuck p.20, also *Kelly's Directory* 1850.
14. Susan Cabell Djabri, 'The Cabell Tomb in Buckfastleigh Chuchyard', *The Devon Historian* 39, October 1989. Also by the same author, *The Story of the Sepulchre*, privately published 1989.

Chapter 2. The Town of Buckfastleigh (pages 13-31)

1. W.G. Hoskins, *Devon*, (1954), p.130.
2. *Kelly's Directory* 1850 and received Warren family information.
3. Received family information, also *Totnes Times* 2 February 1935, report of lecture given by Mr Ashton Hamlyn.
4. *Western Morning News*, 21 November 1877.
5. I am grateful to Simon Timms for noting to me a rare surviving census of Buckfastleigh for 1697-8, giving its population as 1,111. See Michael Laithwaite 'Totnes Houses 1500-1800' in Peter Clark (ed.) *The Transformation of English Provincial Towns* (1994) p.97.
6. Warren Family Bible entries and received information.
7. Received information via my maternal grandmother and mother.
8. Written notes left by my maternal grandmother.
9. Clutterbuck p.14.
10. Dates from *White's Directory* (1878). Information re. fair given by my maternal grandmother.
11. This and following details from handwritten notes left by my maternal grandmother.
12. The Revd Robert Bradford to Dean Milles.
13. My maternal grandmother's notes.
14. Correspondence from the late Wilf Joint. His source unknown.
15. I am indebted to Dr. R. R. Sellman, MA, former County Inspector of Schools for Devon, with whom I had correspondence on the subject in 1976, for information on Buckfastleigh schools in the nineteenth century.
16. From Dr Sellman, based on eighteenth century visitation returns.
17. From Dr Sellman, based on parliamentary returns of 1818.
18. From Dr Sellman, based on parliamentary returns of 1833.
19. Devon Record Office. Diocesan/Principal Registry/Basket cc/Box 11/Schools/Replies to Queries 1837/Buckfastleigh.
20. Dom John Stephan OSB *Devon and Cornwall Notes and Queries* XXIX (1962) p.79.
21. Received family information.
22. Correspondence from Dr Sellman. He kindly wrote to me at length but did not quote all sources. Doubtless the figures were from various returns and inspection reports.
23. R.A. Otter ed., *Civil Engineering Heritage*, Southern England, Institution of Civil Engineers (1994).
24. Hoskins, p.151.
25. Michael Hawkins and contributors, *Devon Roads*, Devon Books (1988), pp. 85 and 86.
26. T. L. Stoate, *Devon Hearths Tax 1674* (1982).
27. For photographs of members of the Hamlyn family see Sandra Coleman's *Buckfastleigh: A Town in the Making* privately published (1982).
28. Helen Harris *The Story of St Luke's* (1994).
29. Various inherited contemporary newspaper cuttings, not all accredited.
30. *Western Morning News* article 20 December 1950.
31. Hilary Beard, *Buckfast in Bygone Days* (1991) pp.48-9.
32. Received information included in Harris, *The Industrial Archaeology of Dartmoor* (but only in early editions 1968 and 1971). Also *Western Morning News* 20 December 1950.

Chapter 3. Buckfast Abbey

1. The description of the Abbey's history outlined in this chapter follows closely Robin Clutterbuck's *Buckfast Abbey a History* published by the Buckfast Abbey Trustees (1994).
2. S. W. Brown, 'Excavations and Building Recording at Buckfast Abbey, Devon, *Proceedings of the Devon Archaeological Society 46* (1988), pp. 13-89.

3. Aileen Fox, 'A Monastic Homestead on Dean Moor, South Devon', *Medieval Archaeology 2* (1958), pp. 141-57.
4. The *Totnes Times* 27 August 1932.

Chapter 4. Holy Trinity Church (pages 32-38)

1. I am grateful for this information to Professor Nicholas Orme of the University of Exeter who wrote to me: 'The fraternity of the Trinity is mentioned 1487 (Weaver, *Somerset Medieval Wills vol i*), p.265); the actual dedication of the church in a will of 1518 in PRO, Prob 1/19, f.74. And it is then in Ecton's Thesaurus of 1742, p.170, and most later sources'.
2. Jeremiah Milles, 'Parochial Returns', Bodleian Library MS Top. Devon c.8. Microfilm copy in Westcountry Studies Library, Exeter.
3. For various information in this chapter I have referred closely to the architectural and historical report prepared by Keystone Historic Building Consultants in November 1992. Ref. here p.3. Dr. J. Cox of Keystone Consultants also kindly commented on a draft of this chapter.
4. Keystone, pp. 11-12.
5. Keystone, pp. 13-14.
6. Keystone, pp. 12-13
7. See Appendix 6.
8. Keystone, pp. 42.
9. Keystone, pp. 13.
10. Keystone, pp. 13.
11. Keystone, pp. 13.
12. *Transactions of the Exeter Diocesan Architectural Society* (1848).
13. Keystone, p.14.
14. Keystone, P.15.
15. Harris, *The Story of St Luke's* (1894).
16. Notes received from the late Wilf Joint - sources not identified.
17. Order of service in possession of this author.
18. Correspondence between the Revd John Scott and W. Joint during August 1992, with which Mr Scott also provided transcripts of the Buckfastleigh Wardens' Accounts, 1712-1794, from the Devon Record Office.
19. From inscription on bell as noted in the *Western Guardian* 17 January 1935.
20. Order of service in possession of this author.
21. Buckfastleigh Parochial Church Council Minutes.
22. PCC Minutes of meetings 24 March 1933 and 12 May 1933.
23. PCC Minutes 30 May 1933.
24. PCC Minutes 27 July 1933.
25. PCC Minutes 19 December 1933.
26. PCC Minutes.
27. PCC Minutes 20 November 1934.
28. *Transactions of the Exeter Diocesan Architectural Society* (1848), and Keystone pp.42-3.
29. PCC Minutes 16 November 1931, and newspaper cuttings (unidentified).
30. Order of service in possession of this author.
31. S.R. Blaylock, *Buckfastleigh Chapel Fabric Survey*. Exeter Museum Archaeological Field Unit Report No 91.13. (March 1991).
32. Djabri, *The Story of the Sepulchre* (1989) p.7.
33. PCC Minutes.
34. PCC Minutes 10 July 1974, and following meeting.

Chapter 5. The Fire of 1992 (pages 39-53

1. Details about the fire include information gathered from reports in the *Western Morning News, South Devon and Plymouth Times* and the *Mid Devon Advertiser*, from 22 July 1992.

Chapter 6. Holy Trinity in the Life of the Parish (pages 54-74)

1. PCC Minutes 9 February 1939 and 14 July 1939. Also my paternal grandmother's diaries.
2. Note from the Church Commissioners 12 January 1960.
3. J.H.D. Hooper, 'The Caverns of Buckfastleigh' *Transactions of the Devonshire Association 79* (1947) pp. 113-116.
4. Ed. J. Beer, (ed.) *Buckfastleigh Remembered* (1981).

INDEX